WITHDRAWN FROM STOCK

Life in the UK Test 2023

Life in the UK Test 2023

With 500 Official Style Practice Test Questions and Answers – To Ensure You Pass Quickly and Easily

Freddie Ixworth

Ixworth

CONTENTS

1

Introduction

Welcome to the Life in the UK Test 2023. We want to do everything we can to make you pass the test on your first (or next) attempt! We want you to be a happy and successful part of the UK, and this audiobook is going to help you become exactly that.

The Life in the UK Test is, of course, a requirement for international individuals wishing to live in the UK permanently or to apply to become British citizens.

To give you every chance of passing this year, we have prepared 500 official style practise questions for you, with full answers supplied in the second half of the book—to ensure you have the latest materials to study.

The year 2022 was an eventful year in the UK following the passing of Queen Elizabeth II at age 96 and the downfall of Prime Minister Boris Johnson—who resigned after top government officials quit their roles following a series of internal scandals.

The Queen's passing and the succession of King Charles III to the throne stands as one of the biggest developments in recent history for the UK and will certainly impact how you answer questions on the test. From questions about the next heir to the throne to the updated name of the national anthem, which has changed from "God Save the Queen" to "God Save the King", you will need to pay close attention to recent events.

The 500 questions inside are arranged over three different chapters, with questions equally spread across each chapter. The questions are hand-picked from the *Official Life in The United Kingdom: A Guide for New Residents* book—so the material you're learning from is right up to date. Hence, it includes updates related to the UK leaving the European Union and more. The questions are equally spread across history, modern society, law, and your role as a citizen in the United Kingdom. The types of questions you can expect in the test will be in one of the following four formats.

- Selecting one correct answer from four choices
- Choosing whether a statement is true or false
- Choosing which of two different statements is correct
- Selecting two correct answers from four choices

When you take the test, you'll have just 24 questions to answer about important aspects of life in the UK. The test takes place on a computer, and you'll have 45 minutes to complete the test. This gives you almost two minutes to answer each question, so keep this in mind. To give you an idea of the format of this book, we'll present each of the three sections in the same order that you read the guide.

To pass the Life in the UK test, you'll need to answer 18 of the 24 questions correctly, in other words—answer at least 75% of them correctly. So, once you've finished preparing for your test, don't worry if after going through these questions again that there might be a few questions that still leave you baffled!

Once you are ready, book your test online at www.lifeintheuk-test.gov.uk. You will need a credit card or debit card, an email address, and your ID. Your test will be at an approved location; there are more than 30 around the country and you'll receive clear instructions on when and where to be once you book your test. You can book your test up to three days in advance. The test costs £50 and you can take it as many times as you need to until you pass.

Make sure you read all the way to the end as we've included comprehensive lists of sports personalities, kings and queens as well as other additional aspects that you need to remember for the examination.

A Long and Inspiring History

---- Early Britain ----

1) The first people to live in Britain were hunter-gathers, who lived in which age?

A – The Iron Age

B – The Stone Age

C – The Ice Age

D – The Industrial Age

2) How did people in Britain get to the European continent during the Stone Age?

A – By plane

B – By horse

C – By a land bridge

D – By car

3) When did Britain become permanently separated from the continent of Europe?

A – 100 years ago

B – 1,000 years ago

C – 10,000 years ago

D – 100,000 years ago

4) Some of the first farmers arrived in Britain 6,000 years ago, which of the following did they build?
A – Big Ben
B – Buckingham Palace
C – Windsor Castle
D – Stonehenge

5) Which county is the Stonehenge monument located in?
A – Derbyshire
B – Hampshire
C – Lancashire
D – Wiltshire

6) Which country in the British Isles can you find the island, Orkney?
A – England
B – Scotland
C – Wales
D – Northern Ireland

7) True or False: The Bronze Age was followed by the Iron Age.

8) Roughly when was the Bronze Age?
A – 4,000 years ago
B – 2,000 years ago
C – 40,000 years ago
D – 20,000 years ago

9) In which period did people begin to create Britain's first coins and trading economy?
A – The Iron Age

B – The Bronze Age
C – The New Age
D – The Industrial Age

10) **Who led the failed Roman invasion of Britain in 55 BC (before Christ)?**
A – Napoleon
B – Julius Caesar
C – Marcus Aurelius
D – Alexander the Great

11) **The Romans later succeeded in occupying most of Britain, which year did this happen?**
A – 430 AD
B – 43 AD
C – 70 AD
D – 700 AD

12) **The Statue of Boudicca is found where in London?**
A – Chelsea and Kensington
B – Euston Station
C – The Banking District
D – On Westminster Bridge

13) **True or False: Hadrian's Wall protected the area that we now call Scotland from ever being conquered by the Romans.**

14) **During the 400 years the Romans remained in Britain, what did they NOT create?**
A – English food
B – Buildings
C – Laws
D – Roads

15) Did the Romans ever return after leaving the British Isles? Yes or No?

A – No

B – Yes

16) When the Anglo-Saxon Kingdoms were established around 600 AD, which parts of Britain remained mostly free of Anglo-Saxon rule?

A – Wales and Scotland

B – England and Northern Ireland

17) True or False: The languages of the Jutes, Angles, and Saxons (who invaded Britain) formed the basis of the modern English language.

18) Who was the most famous Christian missionary to influence the Anglo-Saxons?

A – St. Patrick, who became the Patron Saint of Ireland

B – St. George

C – St. Mary

D – St. James

19) Who spread Christianity in the south of Britain?

A – St. George

B – St. Augustine

C – Jesus

D – St. Mary

20) Where did the Vikings come from?

A – Mexico

B – Singapore and Indonesia

C – Italy, Spain, and Portugal

D – Denmark, Norway, and Sweden

21) When did the Vikings first raid Britain for goods and slaves?
A – 900 AD
B – 789 AD
C – 200 BC
D – 1000 AD

22) True or False: The Vikings defeated the Anglo-Saxons.

23) Some of the Vikings stayed in Britain in an area called Danelaw in the northeast of England. Which towns can be found there now?
A – Grimsby and Scunthorpe
B – Bolton and Bury
C – New Danelaw and Exeter
D – None of the above

24) The Anglo-Saxons ruled England, except for a short time where Danish Kings ruled. What was the name of the first of these Kings?
A – Cnut
B – Bnut
C – Borgen
D – Eriksen

25) In which year did the Battle of Hastings take place?
A – 1077
B – 1099
C – 1088
D – 1066

26) Which King was killed in the Battle of Hastings, by William, the Duke of Normandy?

A – Harold

B – Churchill

C – George

D – Louis

27) King William became known as:

A – William of the West

B – William the Great One

C – William the Conqueror

D – William Will Do It

28) The Battle of Hastings is commemorated by which piece of art?

A – The Mona Lisa

B – The Bayeux Tapestry

C – The Last Supper

D – View of the Battle of Hastings

29) True or False: The Norman Conquest was the most recent successful foreign invasion of England.

30) True or False: The Normans also conquered Wales.

31) True or False: The Normans conquered Scotland.

32) King William created a list of who owned all the land and the animals that people owned in England. What was this list called?

A – Domesday Book

B – Government Land List

C – Book of Living and Livestock

D – Population of England Book

---- The Middle Ages ----

33) Which period of history does the following section on the Middle Ages focus on?

A – The Roman Empire

B – After the Norman Conquest

C – The Iron Age

D – Before the Norman Conquest

34) In which year did King Edward I of England introduce the state of Rhuddlan, which annexed Wales to the Crown of England?

A – 1066

B – 1928

C – 1755

D – 1284

35) In which country in Britain can you find the Castle of Caernarvon and the Castle of Conwy?

A – Northern Ireland

B – Wales

C – Scotland

D – England

36) True or False: The last of the Welsh rebellions were defeated in the 16th Century.

37) Scotland fought England and again was not conquered in the Battle of Bannockburn in 1314. Who was the battle led by on the Scotland side?

A – James the Bruce

B – Richard the Bruce

C – Robert the Bruce

D – Vivienne the Bruce

38) Around the year 1200, the English ruled an area then known as Pale. Which city is it now known as?

A – Ipswich

B – Bristol

C – Glasgow

D – Dublin

39) How long did the Hundred Years' War last?

A – 100 years

B – 103 years

C – 116 years

D – 130 years

40) Who was involved in the Hundred Years' War?

A – England and Ireland

B – England and France

C – England and Spain

D – England and Argentina

41) In which war did King Henry V's English army heavily defeat the French army?

A – The Battle of Agincourt

B – The Battle of Hastings

C – The Battle of Trafalgar

D – The Second Battle of Trafalgar

42) True or False: The English mostly left France in the 1450s.

43) The system of Kings giving land to Lords is called what?

A – Socialism

B – Capitalism

C – Communism

D – Feudalism

44) In the north of Scotland, a different system was operated, where land was owned by members of the what?
A – Slaves
B – Clans
C – Feuds
D – Serfs

45) What was the Black Death?
A – A form of plague
B – A virus
C – Mass genocide
D – Mass suicide

46) How much of the English, Scottish, and Welsh population died during the plague?
A – 10%
B – 20%
C – Around 30%
D – 50%

47) True or False: The plague led to excess labour and falling wages.

48) True or False: Before 1215 the King's power was absolute, it was only after 1215 that the King (John) was forced by his noblemen to agree to some of their requests.

49) The result of this limited power led to which charter of rights agreement?
A – The Constitution
B – Magna Carta
C – Holy Grail

D – The Privacy Law

50) What was the function of the Magna Carta?
A – To restrict the rights of the King to collect taxes or change laws
B – To allow the Kings to collect more taxes and change laws
C – To allow the Kings to set new borders
D – To allow common people to vote

51) As more people joined Parliament, two separate houses were created. What were these houses called and are still called today?
A – The House of Nobles and the House of Bishops
B – The House of Lords and the House of Commons
C – The House and the Slope
D – The First House and the Second House

52) True or False: Scotland also had two houses in their Parliament.

53) What was introduced in the legal system by the Judges in England at this time?
A – Gay Rights
B – Women's Rights
C – Anti-Trust Law
D – Common Law

54) True or False: Scotland also applied Common Law during this period.

55) At this point in time in the Middle Ages (after the Norman Conquest in the 1200s), what language did the King and his people speak?
A – French
B – English
C – Anglo-Saxon (also known as 'Old English')

D – Finnish

56) What language did the peasants speak at this same time?
A – French
B – English
C – Anglo-Saxon (also known as 'Old English')
D – Finnish

57) True or False: Eventually, these languages merged to become what we know as English, with some Anglo-Saxon words and other words from French.

58) True or False: By 1400, official papers in the Parliament were being written in the English language.

59) Geoffrey Chaucer's series of poems about a pilgrimage is called what?
A – The Chaucer Tales
B – The Canterbury Tales
C – Journey to the East
D – The Long Journey

60) Who was the first person to print books in England using a printing press?
A – William Caxton
B – King Harold
C – King Henry
D – Geoffrey Chaucer

61) During this time (around the 1400s) in Scotland, which language was mostly spoken?
A – Anglo-Saxon
B – Gaelic

C – French

D – English

62) John Barber, a poet in Scotland wrote 'The Bruce' about which battle?

A – The Battle of Bannockburn

B – The Battle of Hastings

C – The Battle of Trafalgar

D – The Wars of the Roses

63) During the Middle Ages, which kind of buildings were built?

A – Skyscrapers

B – Mud and sand huts

C – Townhouses

D – Castles and cathedrals

64) True or False: Windsor Castle and Edinburgh Castle are no longer in use.

65) During the Middle Ages, England was heavily involved in trading with other countries. Which of the following was a famous export from England?

A – Gold

B – Oil

C – Wool

D – Coal

66) Foreigners also came from continental Europe to England for work. Where did the weavers come from?

A – France

B – Germany

C – Holland

D – Italy

67) Foreigners also came from Europe to England for work. Where did the engineers come from?

A – France

B – Germany

C – Holland

D – Italy

68) Where did the glassmakers come from?

A – France

B – Germany

C – Holland

D – Italy

69) Where did the canal builders come from?

A – France

B – Germany

C – Holland

D – Italy

70) In the year 1455, which civil war began to decide the King of England?

A – The Battle of Bannockburn

B – The Battle of Hastings

C – The First World War

D – The Wars of the Roses

71) True or False: The Wars of the Roses was fought between the House of Commons and the House of Lords.

72) What is the symbol of the House of Lancaster?

A – A red rose

B – A white rose

C – A tree

D – A lion

73) **What is the symbol of the House of York?**

A – A red rose

B – A white rose

C – A tree

D – A lion

74) **The end of the Wars of the Roses was in which year, signified by The Battle of Bosworth Field?**

A – 1428

B – 1479

C – 1499

D – 1485

75) **True or False: King Richard III was killed in battle at Bosworth Field.**

76) **Who succeeded King Richard III after his death?**

A – King Henry VII

B – Elizabeth of York

C – King Richard IV

D – Queen Victoria

77) **After King Henry VII married Elizabeth of York (which united the two families), what was the new symbol of the House of Tudor?**

A – A red rose

B – A white rose

C – Three roses

D – A red rose with a white rose inside

---- The Tudors and Stuarts ----

78) **What did King Henry VII do after his victory in the Wars of the Roses?**
A – Allocated more power to the nobles
B – Lost some of the financial reserves
C – Reduced the power of the nobles
D – Changed his name to King Henry VIII

79) **When Henry VII died, his son (Henry VIII) continued the reign of power, but what was Henry VIII most famous for?**
A – Leaving the church of Rome and having six wives
B – For growing vegetables in his castle gardens
C – Waging foreign wars
D – Economic reforms

80) **King Henry VIII died of which cause?**
A – Death in battle
B – Obesity and physical decline
C – Extreme old age
D – Murder by an assassin

81) **Who was the first wife of Henry VIII?**
A – Anne Boleyn
B – Anne of Cleves
C – Catherine Parr
D – Catherine of Aragon

82) Why did Henry decide to annul (declare the marriage had no legal existence) his first wife Catherine of Aragon, without the approval of the Pope?

A – To go against the Pope who he disliked

B – To find another wife who could give him a son and be heir to the throne

C – To live the rest of his life single

D – His wife did not respect his religion

83) True or False: Henry VIII's second wife (Anne Boleyn) was executed at the Tower of London as she was said to have taken lovers.

84) True or False: Henry VIII's third wife (Jane Seymour) gave Henry the heir to the throne that he was looking for.

85) Why did Henry VIII marry his fourth wife (Anne of Cleves)?

A – For money

B – For a son

C – Because he fell in love with her

D – For political reasons

86) What was the fate of Henry VIII's wife (Catherine Howard)?

A – She fell off her horse

B – She was executed for taking lovers

C – She fell from the roof of the castle

D – She died of the plague

87) The final wife of Henry VIII was a widow named Catherine Parr. Who died first, her or King Henry VIII?

A – Catherine Parr

B – King Henry VII

88) When the Pope did not allow King Henry VIII to divorce his first wife, what did Henry do?

A – He established the Church of England

B – He murdered the Pope

89) As England and the rest of Europe moved from Roman Catholic to the Church of England, what was this transition called?

A – The Resurrection

B – Feudalism

C – Socialism

D – The Reformation

90) True or False: The Protestants formed their own churches where they did not pray to saints or shrines.

91) True or False: Protestant culture lost strength in England, Wales, and Scotland during the 16th Century.

92) Over in Ireland, English attempts to impose Protestant rule led to violent rebellion by which Irish group?

A – The Pales

B – The Chieftains

93) What did Henry VIII accomplish during his time as King?

A – He united Wales with England

B – He united Ireland with England

C – He united Scotland with England

D – He united France with England

94) Who was King Henry VIII succeeded after his death?

A – Queen Elizabeth I

B – Queen Mary, known as Bloody Mary

C – King Edward VI

D – King Henry IX

95) At what age did King Edward VI die?
A – 15
B – 19
C – 25
D – 40

96) Which book was written during Edward VI's rule in Britain?
A – The Canterbury Tales
B – The Book of Common Prayer
C – The Bible
D – The Prince

97) True or False: After King Edward VI's death, his half-sister Mary took the throne.

98) True or False: Queen Mary was succeeded by Elizabeth, the youngest offspring of Henry VIII and his second wife.

99) What was Queen Elizabeth I's religious preference?
A – Roman Catholic
B – Protestant
C – Atheist
D – Jewish

100) How did Queen Elizabeth I allow for religious harmony in England?
A – She appreciated the views of both the Catholics and the Protestants
B – She did not ask about people's real beliefs

101) Why was Elizabeth I such a popular monarch?
A – She gave people money

B – She gave people land

C – She gave people livestock

D – She defeated the Spanish Armada (a fleet of ships) in 1588

102) **Over in Scotland, the mostly Protestant Parliament also abolished the Pope's authority and Roman Catholic services were made illegal by law. Who was the Queen of Scotland at this time?**

A – Mary Stuart, now also known as 'Mary, Queen of Scots'

B – Queen Elizabeth I

C – Queen Victoria

D – Queen Olivia

103) **True or False: After returning from France to Scotland, Mary was suspected to be involved in the murder of her husband. She then fled to England, giving the throne to her Protestant son James VI of Scotland.**

104) **What was the fate of Mary when she arrived in England?**

A – She took the throne in England

B – She was held prisoner for 20 years, and later executed by Queen Elizabeth I

C – She became an English citizen

D – She gave birth to another son

105) **The Elizabethan era was a time of what in England?**

A – Violent war

B – Pride of being English

C – New architecture

D – New culinary tastes

106) **Who was Sir Francis Drake?**

A – Son to Elizabeth I

B – A founder of England's naval tradition

C – A famous pirate

D – A famous cricket player

107) What was the name of the ship Sir Francis Drake sailed around the world?

A – The Conqueror

B – The Drake

C – The Silver Hind

D – The Golden Hind

108) During Elizabeth I's reign, which region did English settlers begin to colonise?

A – Eastern coast of America

B – Eastern coast of India

C – Eastern coast of Australia

D – Eastern coast of Italy

109) The Elizabethan era is also fondly recollected for poetry. Which of the following is a famous English poet and playwriter?

A – Mrs. Mansouri

B – Francis Drake

C – William Shakespeare

D – Justin Timberlake

110) Where was William Shakespeare born?

A – Richmond, London

B – Avonmouth, Bristol

C – Stratford-upon-Avon

D – Sefton Park, Merseyside

111) Which of the following is not a poem or play written by William Shakespeare?

A – Roses

B – Hamlet

C – A Midsummer Night's Dream

D – Romeo and Juliet

112) Shakespeare was one of the first poets to do what?

A – Portray women

B – Portray same-sex romance

C – Include ordinary English men and women

D – Have a book printed on the printing press

113) William Shakespeare was born in 1564 and died in what year?

A – 1616

B – 1717

C – 1669

D – 1600

114) True or False: Shakespeare's plays and poems are still studied today across many schools in Britain.

115) In which London Theatre is a modern take of Shakespeare's plays still performed today?

A – The Globe Theatre

B – The Trafalgar Theatre

116) True or False: When Queen Elizabeth I died, Elizabeth II took the throne.

117) What was the main achievement or notable production of King James I's time in power?

A – Creation of the car

B – Creation of the airplane

C – Creation of canals

D – Creation of the King James Bible

118) True or False: Protestant settlements during this time in Ireland were known as plantations.

119) King James I's son was called what name?
A – Charles I
B – James II

120) Why did the Scottish army rebel against Charles I?
A – Because he disrespected Scotland
B – Because he attempted to introduce a prayer book to the Presbyterian Church

121) After the Civil War began in 1642, the country split into which two sets of people – The Cavaliers and the Roundheads. Who did the Cavaliers support?
A – The Parliament
B – The Kings

122) Charles I's army was defeated in 1646 in which battle(s)?
A – The Battle of Bannockburn
B – The Battle of Hastings
C – The Battle of Marston Moor and Battle of Naseby
D – The Battle of Trafalgar

123) Charles I was held by the Parliament's army and executed in which year?
A – 1659
B – 1649
C – 1669
D – 1679

124) After the execution, England became a republic. What was it called?

A – The Monarchy

B – The United Kingdom

C – The British Isles

D – The Commonwealth

125) One of the generals in the army at this time, Oliver Cromwell, became famed for what during his successful power grab in the English Parliament?

A – For being so charming

B – For being so clever

C – For being so funny

D – For being so violent

126) When Charles II's Scottish army attacked England, Cromwell defeated them. Where did Charles II famously hide during his escape from Worcester?

A – Inside a tree

B – Inside a fishing boat

C – Inside a peasant's home

D – Inside a cave

127) After his success, Cromwell was named leader of the republic and was called Lord Protector. Who succeeded him after his death in 1658?

A – His son, Richard

B – His daughter, Lottie

128) Sadly, Richard was not such a great leader as Oliver Cromwell and people demanded that a King be restored. Who returned from Europe (Holland) and was crowned King of England, Wales, Scotland, and Ireland in 1660?

A – Charles II
B – Charles III
C – Henry IX
D – Henry X

129) Was this the only known period of time that England was a republic?
A – Yes
B – No

130) True or False: This time, Charles II would cooperate with Parliament and the Church of England again became the official Church.

131) During Charles II's reign, which major event happened in 1666?
A – The Black Death
B – The Spanish Flu
C – World War I
D – The Great Fire of London

132) Which landmark in London was famously rebuilt after this great fire?
A – Buckingham Palace
B – The House of Parliament
C – St. Paul's Cathedral
D – Chelsea Bridge

133) In 1679, which important act was introduced?
A – The Magna Carta
B – The Habeas Corpus
C – The Children's Act
D – The People's Act

134) Charles II was also interested in science and helped to create the Royal Society. Which well-known individual originated from that society?

A – The Duke of Sussex

B – Isaac Newton

C – David Beckham

D – JP Morgan

135) What scientific principle did Isaac Newton famously discover and demonstrate?

A – Thermodynamics

B – Particle energy

C – Gravity

D – The spinning ball earth

136) Isaac Newton studied at which university?

A – Cambridge University

B – Sheffield University

C – Oxford University

D – Bath University

137) In 1685, Charles II (who had no children) died. Who was given the throne?

A – His brother, James

B – His brother, Hugo

138) Which religion did King James II favour?

A – The Church of England

B – Roman Catholic

C – Paganism

D – Puritanism

139) Why did people stop worrying that England would become a Catholic country under James II?

A – Because he was not forceful

B – Because his daughters (heirs) were Protestant

C – Because the will of the people was strong

D – Because Catholicism was losing popularity across the rest of Europe

140) True or False: The Glorious Revolution was "glorious" because there was no fighting.

141) What did the Glorious Revolution achieve?

A – It led to many peasants leaving the country

B – It meant there was no threat of the Monarchy having total control

C – Integration with the rest of Europe

D – Widespread technological innovation

142) True or False: After William of Orange invaded England during the Glorious Revolution, James fled to France. Later he wanted to regain the throne, so he attacked Ireland with the help of a French army and won the battle of Boyne in 1960.

143) James still had some supporters in Scotland and even in England. What did his supporters become known as?

A – The Jameses

B – The Nationals

C – The Jacobites

D – The Scots

---- A Global Power ----

144) At the coronation of William and Mary, which bill was written in 1689?

A – The Bill of Rights
B – The Privacy Act
C – The Women's Act
D – The Slave's Act

145) What did the Bill of Rights achieve?
A – Further limits to the King's power
B – More power to the Monarchy
C – Peace in Europe
D – Religious freedom

146) True or False: The Parliament decided that each new King or Queen must be
Catholic.

147) The bill concluded that a new parliament had to be elected every three years, which later changed to every seven years. How many years must a parliament be re-elected today?
A – 3
B – 5
C – 7
D – 9

148) These changes (as well as navy and army funding) meant that the Monarch required ministers to vote in the House of Commons and the House of Lords. Which were the two main groups in Parliament at this time?
A – The Liberal Democrats and the Tories
B – The Liberal Democrats and the Green Party
C – The Whigs and the Green Party
D – The Whigs and the Tories

149) True or False: The Whigs are now referred to as the Conservative Party.

150) This was a new time, a time of party politics. What else was also new at this
time?
A – Freedom of movement
B – Freedom of banking
C – Freedom of speech
D – Freedom of the press

151) Which year was the freedom of the press introduced, where newspapers no longer needed a license to operate and publish their news?
A – 1693
B – 1694
C – 1695
D – 1696

152) True or False: After the Glorious Revolution, the British Isles was called a 'constitutional monarchy', where the King or Queen was still important but couldn't pass new laws if Parliament didn't agree.

153) True or False: This was now a time of democracy where anybody could vote on laws and bills in Parliament.

154) The population in Britain increased between 1650 and 1720, where did refugees arrive from?
A – Jerusalem and France (The Jews and Huguenots)
B – Eastern Europe and Africa
C – India
D – China

155) Who was the successor of William III of England and William II of Scotland?

A – William IV

B – Queen Anne, who had no children of her own

C – Queen Elizabeth

D – Queen Victoria

156) Since Queen Anne had no airs to the throne in England, Wales, Scotland, and Ireland, which act was created in 1707?

A – The Bill of Rights

B – The Privacy Act

C – The Women's Act

D – The Acts of Union (which created the United Kingdom of Great Britain, meaning Scotland was no longer an independent land)

157) Queen Anne died in 1714, who did Parliament choose to be the next King?

A – A German, George I

B – James II

C – Edward II

D – Charles I

158) Why was the first Prime Minister (Sir Robert Walpole) established in 1721?

A – Because George I was not accomplishing much

B – Because there was social unrest and violence

C – Because George I did not speak good English

D – Because there were protests about democracy

159) Until which year did the first Prime Minister control the United Kingdom?

A – 1728

B – 1738

C – 1742

D – 1753

160) Which rebellion occurred in 1745?

A – The Rebellion of Ireland

B – The Rebellion of the Monarchy

C – The Rebellion of the People

D – The Rebellion of the Scottish Clans

161) True or False: Charles Edward Stuart (otherwise called Bonnie Prince Charlie) lost the Battle of Culloden against George II (George I's son) in 1746 during the Rebellion of the Clans.

162) True or False: The clans became landlords and the chieftains became their paying tenants.

163) During the 'Highland Clearances', small farms or crofts were destroyed by landlords to make way for what?

A – Fields of sheep and cows

B – Fields of hay

C – Fields of chickens

D – Fields of vegetables

164) Who was Robert Burns?

A – A famous Scottish King

B – A famed criminal

C – The first Scottish footballer

D – A famous Scottish poet

165) The Enlightenment happened during the 18th Century. What did this involve?

A – People became interested in politics, philosophy, and science

B – People became interested in spirituality, yoga, and meditation

C – People returned to more traditional beliefs

D – The explosion of a new religion

166) Which idea from the Enlightenment era is still valid in today's day and age?

A – The idea that everyone should be entitled to their own religious or political view

B – Ideas about the Earth as flat

C – Equal rights for men and woman

D – Acceptance of foreign immigration

167) Before the 18th Century, agriculture was the biggest source of employment in Britain. Which of the following became the biggest source of employment during the 18th and 19th Century?

A – Finance

B – Fashion

C – Sports

D – Industrials

168) True or False: Britain was the first country to industrialise, or to use machinery and steam power on a large scale.

169) True or False: Steel production led to a huge rise in ships and railway building and the manufacturing industry became the main source of jobs in Britain.

170) What was Richard Arkwright known for?

A – His poetry

B – His carding machine and efficiency in running factories

C – His governing skill

D – His violent tendencies

171) How were the working conditions during the Industrial Revolution?

A – Extremely pleasant

B – Very poor

C – Mostly unknown

D – Better than the modern day

172) During these years, Britain also colonised many peoples in Canada, India, Africa, and other regions. Which countries did Britain import textiles, tea, and spices from?

A – North America and The West Indies

B – India and Indonesia

C – Argentina

D – Australia

173) Who mapped the coast of Australia?

A – James Cook

B – James Bond

C – Charles Darwin

D – Sir Edmund Hillary

174) What did Sake Dean Mahomet open in London in 1810?

A – The first supermarket

B – The first curry house

C – The first Bengal Society

D – The first Bengal army

175) True or False: At this time, the slave trade was legal in Britain.

176) True or False: In the late 1700s, the Quakers opposed the slave trade and

the terrible living conditions that the slaves were put under. This, as well as the abolitionists, helped to free the slaves and by 1807 it was illegal to trade slaves in British ships and British ports.

177) In which year was the Emancipation Act (which abolished slavery throughout the British Empire) established?

A – 1807

B – 1818

C – 1822

D – 1833

178) Some of the original British families colonised North America because they wanted religious freedom and believed in liberty. Why did they begin to feel frustrated by the British government?

A – When the government imposed freedom of speech laws

B – When the government demanded they return to Britain

C – When the government tried to tax them

D – When the government imposed travel restrictions

179) Fighting broke out as the colonialists felt there should be 'no taxation without representation', so in 1776 how many colonies declared their independence?

A – 13

B – 24

C – 11

D – 7

180) The colonists eventually defeated the British Army and the colonies became recognised as independent in 1783. Where were these 13 colonies located?

A – The east coast of America (now New York, Maryland, etc.)

B – The west coast of America (now California, Arizona, etc.)

181) During the 1700s, Britain fought many wars with which country?

A – Germany

B – Holland

C – Italy

D – France

182) True or False: During the French Revolution, the British defeated French and Spanish ships therefore winning the Battle of Trafalgar in 1805, with Nelson's Column in Trafalgar Square a tribute to the then leader of the British Navy.

183) True or False: The Duke of Wellington was killed in battle by the French emperor Napoleon in 1815.

184) Which symbol recognises the union of the United Kingdom of Great Britain and Ireland?

A – The Cross of St. George

B – The Union Jack

C – The Cross of St. Patrick

D – The Welsh Dragon Flag

185) Why are there no aspects of the Welsh flag appearing on the Union Jack?

A – Wales opted out

B – Wales was already united with England when the first Union Jack flag was designed in 1606

186) Who was made Queen in 1837 at the age of just 18?

A – Queen Victoria

B – Queen Anne

C – Queen Elizabeth

D – Queen Fijn

187) Victoria was Queen for almost 64 years. This period was a time of increasing power and financial opulence known as:
A – The Stone Age
B – The Bronze Age
C – The Victorian Age
D – The Empire Age

188) During Victoria's rule, the British Empire expanded to have a population of roughly how many people?
A – 40 million
B – 400 million
C – 1.3 billion
D – 130 million

189) True or False: Working conditions and trading laws improved during the 1800s, including women's and children's working hours, which were limited to 10 hours per day.

190) What is Isambard Kingdom Brunel famously known for?
A – Constructing the Great Western Railway
B – Creating carding factories
C – Politics
D – Social justice

191) During the 19th Century, Britain was the leader of the world when it came to the
iron and coal industries. Which industry did it also become a leader in at this time?
A – TV production
B – Fashion
C – Sports

D – Financial services like banking and investing

192) Who were Britain's allies during the Crimean War in 1853 and 1856?

A – Spain and Belgium

B – Turkey and France

C – Russia and France

D – Russia and Turkey

193) What was Florence Nightingale's (1820 to 1910) occupation?

A – A poet

B – A nurse

C – A pilot

D – A soldier

194) Over in Ireland, things were not so good. The majority of the population were farmers and most depended on potatoes. Which event happened famously?

A – The Irish Plague, killing 1 million people

B – The Great Fire of Dublin, killing 4,000 people

C – The Potato Famine, killing 1 million people

D – The Irish Civil War, killing 400,000 people

195) In 1832, the Reform Act gave more people the right to vote – mostly people in middle-class towns. In 1867, another reform allowed yet more people to vote, but still only property owners and not women. In 1870 and 1882, new rules gave women the right to own what?

A – Earnings and property

B – Jewellery and livestock

C – Book copyrights

D – Slaves

196) Which famous 'suffragette' was influential in giving women voting powers in 1928?

A – Emily Bronte

B – Emmeline Pankhurst

C – Amelia Earhart

D – Emmeline B. Wells

197) What was the 'suffragettes' approach to achieving what they wanted?

A – Sexual appeal

B – Arson and hunger strikes

C – Strong debating

D – Blackmail

198) Why did people begin to question the expansion of the British Empire?

A – They thought it was a drain on national resources

B – The Boer War of 1899 to 1902 was unsuccessful

C – They missed the old times

D – They felt guilt for occupying other countries

199) Who wrote the poem 'If', as well as the Jungle Book story?

A – Mary Stellar

B – Rudyard Kipling

C – Ian Fleming

D – Jane Austin

---- The 20th Century----

200) True or False: As a powerful nation, Britain began social pro-grammes to support various groups such as the poor, divorced women, and unemployed, while pensions were also introduced.

201) Which event cut short this time of prosperity and peace in 1914?

A – World War I

B – World War II

C – The French Revolution

D – The Scottish Crumbling

202) True or False: Britain was allied with powers from around the world including Japan, Serbia, Greece, and Italy.

203) True or False: Around 400,000 Indians were killed during the First World War.

204) The war included more than two million British casualties in total. How many British casualties were there on the first day of the Battle of the Somme in 1916?

A – 1 million

B – 100,000

C – 200,000

D – 60,000

205) At 11am on which day in 1918 did World War 1 end?

A – March 11

B – November 11

C – October 11

D – July 11

206) What happened in 1922 in Ireland?

A – The Potato Famine

B – The Partition of Ireland

C – Reunion of the North and the South

D – A national revolution

207) **What is the violence in Ireland referred to, between those who wanted to remain with the British Government and those who wanted to continue the republic?**

A – The Troubles

B – The Infights

208) **Between the First and Second World Wars, which major event happened?**

A – The Potato Famine

B – The Spanish Flu

C – The Great Depression

D – The Middle War

209) **True or False: Car ownership doubled in Britain in the years between 1930 and 1939.**

210) **True or False: Winston Churchill became the Leader of Britain's war after Adolph Hitler invaded Poland and nearby countries in May 1940.**

211) **Is Winston Churchill an admired leader or a hated leader?**

A – Admired

B – Hated

212) **Churchill also wrote famous speeches which are still repeated today, how many times did he serve as Prime Minister?**

A – 1

B – 2

C – 2

D – 4

213) When the British evacuated France during the evacuation of Dunkirk, who helped to rescue them?

A – Volunteer boat owners and fishermen

B – The Monarchy

C – The government

D – Irish soldiers

214) Which phrase is used to describe the British spirit of pulling together during the heavy airside bombings of East London and Coventry?

A – Spitfire spirit

B – The Blitz spirit

C – The London spirit

D – The ANZAC spirit

215) True or False: Allied forces (including the USA and others) helped to secure victory on the beaches of Normandy, France – referred to as D-Day – and defeated Germany in May 1945.

216) True or False: The war against Japan ended because the Japanese were tired of fighting.

217) What did Alexander Fleming achieve?

A – He created toothpaste

B – He created the pie

C – He discovered penicillin

D – He created the atomic bomb

---- Britain Since 1945 ----

218) Britain had won the war, but at what cost? Its resources were depleted and led to what?

A – The welfare state and labour

B – The Liberal Democrat Party

219) Which social programme was NOT created at this time?
A – The National Health Service

B – Social security

C – Free alcohol for all

D – Railway/gas/electricity nationalisation

220) What is the correct abbreviation for the North Atlantic Treaty Organisation?
A – NATO

B – NTO

C – NAT

D – ATO

221) Clement Attlee, Prime Minister between 1945 and 1951 was a member of which political party?
A – Liberal Democrats

B – Labour

C – Conservative

D – Green Party

222) William Beverage, Liberal MP, is best known for what?
A – The Social Insurance and Allied Services Report

B – Creating the first fizzy beverage

C – Educational reforms

D – Corruption whistle-blower

223) Lord Richard Austen Butler introduced which social reform in 1944?
A – Free after-school clubs

B – Free university in England and Wales

C – Free school meals

D – Free secondary school in England and Wales

224) Why were migrants from the West Indies, India, Pakistan, and Bangladesh encouraged to come to work in the UK?

A – Because there was still a labour shortage in the UK

B – Because they heard the weather was better in the British Isles

C – Free travel

D – Free housing

225) Which word was used to describe the 1960s?

A – The Savage Sixties

B – The Saucy Sixties

C – The Swinging Sixties

D – The Sultry Sixties

226) Which of the following was NOT a feature of the 1960s?

A – Pop music

B – The Concorde

C – High-rise buildings

D – Rapid globalization

227) Which 20th Century British invention was invented by John Logie Beard?

A – Radar

B – The Turing Machine

C – Hovercraft

D – Television

228) Who discovered the structure of the DNA molecule in London and Cambridge?

A – Francis Crick

B – Bernard Lovell

C – John Mcleod

D – Tim Berners-Lee

229) True or False: The Concorde, a supersonic aircraft that was faster than the speed of sound, was retired from service in 2003 and never resumed.

230) What did James Goodfellow invent?

A – Cloning

B – Diesel engines

C – The world wide web

D – The ATM

231) Which of these was not an inherent national problem in the 1970s?

A – Price of goods increasing

B – Strikes and trade union issues

C – Violence in Northern Ireland

D – The English football team not retaining the World Cup

232) Mary Peters was a talented:

A – Athlete

B – Author

C – Nurse

D – Engineer

233) In which year did the UK join the European Union?

A – 1994

B – 1997

C – 1999

D – 1993

LIFE IN THE UK TEST 2023

234) The UK decided not to use the Euro currency, what do we use instead?
A – The Yen
B – The US Dollar
C – The Indonesian Rupiah
D – The Great British Pound Sterling

235) The UK formally left the European Union, when?
A – December 31, 2021
B – January 31, 2020

236) True or False: Margaret Thatcher was the first female Prime Minister, she was a member of the Conservative Party, and the longest serving Prime Minister in the 20th Century.

237) True or False: Margaret Thatcher is disliked by some because she influenced the decline of traditional coal mining and ship-building industries.

238) In 1982, which country invaded the Falkland Islands during Margaret Thatcher's time as Prime Minister?
A – Spain
B – Argentina
C – Great Britain
D – The United States

239) Following Prime Minister Thatcher, John Major became the new Prime Minister – what did he help to restore?
A – Peace in Northern Ireland
B – The coal and shipping industries

240) Roald Dahl is most well-known for writing which books?
A – Children's stories

B – Adults' stories

C – Poems

D – Sci-fi books

241) From 1997 who was elected from the Labour Party until 2007?

A – John Major

B – Ed Balls

C – Gordon Brown

D – Tony Blair

242) What did Tony Blair notably introduce before he was replaced by Gordon Brown in 2007?

A – Free gym memberships

B – University tuition fees

C – Free primary schools

D – The Scottish Parliament and The Welsh Assembly

243) True or False: No political party won the majority vote in 2010.

244) True or False: On June 23, 2016, the UK voted by a margin of 51.9% to 48.1% to remain in the European Union.

3

A Thriving Society and The UK Today

---- The UK Today ----

245) What is the significance of Land's End and John O'Groats?

A – They are capital cities

B – It represents the longest distance between two points on the mainland of the UK

C – Porridge and toast were first invented in those locations

D – They were the first established towns in the UK

246) What is the distance between Land's End and John O'Groats?

A – 140 kilometres

B – 1,400 kilometres

247) What is the capital city of Scotland?

A – Glasgow

B – Edinburgh

C – Falkirk

D – Aberdeen

248) What is the capital city of Wales?

A – Newport
B – Abersoch
C – Swansea
D – Cardiff

249) What is the only currency of the United Kingdom?
A – GBP
B – USD
C – CAD
D – EURO

250) True or False: There is a 3-pence coin in the UK.

251) True or False: There is a 1-pound note in the UK.

252) True or False: There is a 5-pound coin in the UK.

253) True or False: There is a 50-pound note in the UK.

254) In different parts of the UK there are many languages and dialects, does Wales have its own language?
A – No
B – Yes, and it is taught in their schools – however many also speak English

255) Which language is also commonly spoken alongside English, in Scotland?
A – Welsh
B – Gaelic
C – Old English
D – French

256) Which language is also commonly spoken alongside English, in Northern Ireland?

A – Gaelic

B – Irish Gaelic

C – Welsh

D – French

257) What is the population of the UK as of 2022?

A – 70 million

B – 68 million

C – 50 million

D – 100 million

258) What was the population of the UK in 1801?

A – 8 million

B – 30 million

C – 40 million

D – 6 million

259) Which two factors have NOT led to population growth increasing during more recent years?

A – Migration from other countries

B – Couples being offered government money to have children

C – Longer life expectancy

D – Basketball players having more children

260) True or False: The population of the UK is evenly distributed across England, Scotland, Wales, and Northern Ireland?

261) True or False: Manchester has the greatest number of inhabitants.

262) **Britain has an aging population, who are living longer. What does this directly impact?**

A – Cost of pensions and health care

B – Cost of stocks

C – National security

D – Inequality

263) **True or False: COVID-19 has had significant and unequal effects depending on where in the UK people live, their level of education, socioeconomic status, and health.**

264) **Is it a legal requirement that men and women are not discriminated against because of their gender, their working status, or for any other reason?**

A – Yes

B – No

265) **Is it true that women in Britain comprise around half of the workforce, and on average leave high school with more qualifications than male graduates?**

A – Yes

B – No

---- Religion ----

266) **The UK is historically Christian. As of the 2011 Census, which was the largest identifying religion at 59% of the population?**

A – Christian

B – Sikh

C – Buddhist

D – Hindu

267) True or False: There are various religious buildings across the UK, such as churches, mosques, temples, gurdwaras, and others.

268) True or False: Everyone has the legal right to choose to practise any religion, and also to practise no religion.

269) The Church of England is also known as:
A – Christian Orthodox
B – Catholicism
C – The Anglican Church
D – The Church of Jesus Christ of Latter-Day Saints

270) Who is the head of the Church of England?
A – The Prime Minister
B – The Monarchy
C – The Archbishop of Canterbury
D – The Mayor of Oxford

271) Who governs the Church of Scotland (otherwise known as the Presbyterian Church)?
A – Ministers and Elders
B – The Archbishop of Canterbury
C – The Prime Minister
D – The Monarchy

272) Who governs the established official Welsh and Northern Irish Churches?
A – The Monarchy
B – The Archbishop of Canterbury
C – Ministers and Elders
D – There is no established church in these two countries

273) Which is the other biggest denomination of Christianity in the British Isles, aside from the Church of England (Anglican Church)?
A – Roman Catholic
B – Orthodox
C – Evangelical
D – Quakers

274) Which is the Patron Saint Day of England?
A – St. George's Day, on the 23rd of April
B – St. David's Day, on the 1st of March
C – St. Patrick's Day, on the 17th of March
D – St. Andrew's Day, on the 30th of November

275) Which is the Patron Saint Day of Wales?
A – St. George's Day, on the 23rd of April
B – St. David's Day, on the 1st of March
C – St. Patrick's Day, on the 17th of March
D – St. Andrew's Day, on the 30th of November

276) Which is the Patron Saint Day of Scotland?
A – St. George's Day, on the 23rd of April
B – St. David's Day, on the 1st of March
C – St. Patrick's Day, on the 17th of March
D – St. Andrew's Day, on the 30th of November

277) Which is the Patron Saint Day of Northern Ireland?
A – St. George's Day, on the 23rd of April
B – St. David's Day, on the 1st of March
C – St. Patrick's Day, on the 17th of March
D – St. Andrew's Day, on the 30th of November

278) True or False: St. George's Day is an official holiday in England.

---- Customs and Traditions ----

279) On which day does Christmas take place, celebrating the birth of Jesus

Christ?
A – 24th of December
B – 28th of December
C – 26th of December
D – 25th of December

280) Which of the following things is NOT commonly carried out by families in the UK on Christmas day?
A – Eating roast turkey dinner
B – Giving gifts
C – Decorating Christmas trees
D – Going swimming in the morning

281) True or False: Boxing Day is a public holiday that takes place the day before Christmas Day.

282) Which other Christian festival is celebrated in the UK?
A – Easter
B – Halloween
C – Diwali
D – Bonfire Night

283) What is the religious significance of Easter?
A – It marks the coming of the Easter Bunny
B – It marks the death of Jesus Christ on Good Friday and his rising from the dead on Easter Sunday

C – It marks the birth of Jesus Christ

D – The start of a new and prosperous year

284) What food do people typically consume on Shrove Tuesday?

A – Cake

B – Roast dinner

C – Pancakes

D – Toasties

285) The 40 days of Lent (beginning on Ash Wednesday) typically involves what?

A – Giving gifts to each other

B – Reflection and giving up some food types

286) Which gift is given at Easter, sometimes even by non-religious individuals?

A – Easter cakes

B – Easter sausage rolls

C – Easter hot dogs

D – Easter eggs

287) Diwali (the festival of lights) takes place in October or November and lasts for five days. It celebrates the victory of good over evil and the power of knowledge. Which religion is Diwali celebrated by?

A – Protestant Christians

B – Hindus and Sikhs

C – Jews

D – Quakers

288) Hannukah is celebrated in November or December for eight days. Which religion is it celebrated by?

A – Protestant Christians

B – Hindus and Sikhs

C – Jews

D – Quakers

289) Eid al-Fitr celebrates what?

A – Prophet Ibrahim

B – The end of Ramadan

290) Eid ul Adha and Eid al-Fitr are celebrated by which religion?

A – Muslims

B – Hindus and Sikhs

C – Jews

D – Quakers

291) Vaisakhi involves parades, dancing and singing on the 14th of April each year, it is celebrated by which religion?

A – Protestant Christians

B – Sikhs

C – Jews

D – Quakers

292) On which day does Valentine's Day take place in the UK?

A – February 14

B – March 14

C – June 14

D – November 14

293) True or False: Bank holidays have no religious significance, but banks and many other businesses are closed for the day.

294) True or False: Bank holidays take place in May, late May, early June, and August.

295) On which day does April Fool's Day take place?

A – April 1

B – April 8

C – April 13

D – April 31

296) What do children not usually do for their mothers and fathers on Mothering Sunday and Father's Day?

A – Buy cards

B – Buy gifts

C – Cook food

D – Ignore them

297) Bonfire Night takes place on the 5th of November, people set off fireworks and burn large fires. Which 1605 event does this celebrate?

A – Guy Fawkes attempting to burn down the Houses of Parliament

B – The end of the Civil War

C – The end of the 100 Years' War

D – The winning Battle of Trafalgar

298) Remembrance Day, held on the 11th of November each year, is marked by what at 11am?

A – 2 minutes of silence

B – 2 minutes of prayer

C – 5 minutes of silence

D – The national anthem

---- Sports in the UK ----

299) True or False: Many sports such as football, cricket, rugby, tennis, and golf started in Britain.

300) When did the UK most recently host the Olympic and Para-lympic Games in East London?
A – 2000
B – 2010
C – 2020
D – 2012

301) How many times has the UK hosted the Olympic Games?
A – Once
B – Twice
C – Three times
D – Four times

302) What did runner Roger Bannister achieve in 1954?
A – He was the first man to run from Land's End to John O'Groats
B – He ran a marathon in under 2 hours
C – He ran a mile in under 4 minutes
D – He ran a mile in under 10 minutes

303) Ian Botham played which sport?
A – Cricket
B – Football
C – Rowing
D – Rugby

304) Steve Redgrave won gold medals in which sport?
A – Cricket
B – Football
C – Rowing
D – Rugby

305) Dame Kelly Holmes won two gold medals in which sport?

A – Rowing
B – Running
C – Hurdles
D – Tennis

306) Chris Hoy won six Olympic gold medals in which sport?
A – Football
B – Cycling
C – Rowing
D – Rugby

307) Mo Farah is a what?
A – A sprinter
B – A long-distance runner
C – A rugby player
D – A football player

308) Andy Murray is the first British man to win what since 1936?
A – A Tennis Grand Slam
B – An Olympic tennis gold medal
C – The Ballon d'Or
D – The ATP Player Award

309) Ellie Simonds was the youngest Paralympian at which games?
A – 2004
B – 2010
C – 2016
D – 2008

310) The Ashes is a famous cricket tournament featuring a series of matches played against which country?
A – France
B – Canada

C – The West Indies

D – Australia

311) Which is the UK's most popular sport?

A – Rugby

B – Cricket

C – Football

D – Tennis

312) True or False: Many towns and cities in the British Isles have their own teams which they support and there are fierce rivalries between them.

313) In which year did England win the FIFA World Cup?

A – 1977

B – 1966

C – 1955

D – 1944

314) True or False: Rugby has three different official formats, those being Rugby Union, Rugby League, and Rugby Racing.

315) Which is the most well-regarded international rugby tournament in Europe?

A – The Five Nations

B – The Six Nations

C – The Seven Nations

D – The Eight Nations

316) Which British sport holds a strong association with Royalty?

A – Horse racing

B – Tennis

C – Golf

D – Skiing

317) Golf can be traced back to which country and century?
A – 12th Century England
B – 12th Century Scotland
C – 15th Century Scotland
D – 15th Century England

318) Which is the most famous tennis tournament held in Britain?
A – Queen's Club Championships
B – Wimbledon
C – The Ashes
D – FIFA World Cup

319) Sir Robin Knox-Johnston was the first person to do what?
A – Sail around the world, single-handedly
B – Sail around the world, single-handedly and without stopping

320) Recent British Formula 1 winners of the World Championship do not include who?
A – Jenson Button
B – Daniel Riccardo
C – Damon Hill
D – Lewis Hamilton

---- Arts and Culture ----

321) Which eight-week musical event held by the BBC has been running since 1927?
A – The Six Nations
B – Queens
C – The Country Choir Club

D – The Proms

322) Which British classical music composer was the organist at Westminster Abbey?
A – George Handel
B – Henry Purcell
C – Gustav Holst
D – Edward Elgar

323) Who composed 'The Planets'?
A – George Handel
B – Henry Purcell
C – Gustav Holst
D – Edward Elgar

324) Which of these is not an example of a popular summer music festival in the UK?
A – Glastonbury
B – Isle of Wight Festival
C – Strawbury
D – Creamfields

325) True or False: London's west end is also known as 'Theatreland'.

326) In the UK, architecture is both old and beautiful. Many cathedrals from the Middle Ages still stand today in places like Durham, York, Canterbury, and Salisbury. In the late 1600s, which architect helped to envision the new St. Paul's Cathedral after the Great Fire of London?
A – Christopher Wren
B – Inigo Jones
C – Guy Fawkes

D – Arthur Wren

327) In the 18th Century, which architect had a large influence on the city of Bath and the Royal Crescent?
A – Christopher Wren
B – Robert Adam
C – Guy Fawkes
D – Arthur Wren

328) Which famous landscape architect devised the grounds in many country homes, such as Chatsworth House?
A – Inigo Jones
B – Lancelot 'Capability' Brown
C – Guy Fawkes
D – Christopher Wren

329) Which London flower show aired annually on TV showcases garden designs from the British Isles around the world?
A – Streatham Flower Show
B – Brentford Flower Show
C – Chelsea Flower Show
D – Stockwell Flower Show

330) True or False: Many great fashion icons come from the UK, some of these in recent years include Alexander McQueen and Vivienne Westwood.

331) True or False: St Pancras Station as well as town halls in Manchester and Sheffield are built in 'gothic' style architecture.

332) James Bond was introduced in which British author's book series.
A – JRR Tolkien

B – Ian Fleming

C – JK Rowling

D – William Golding

333) Which famous English novelist wrote 'Sense and Sensibility' as well as 'Pride and Prejudice'?

A – Jane Austen

B – Eveleyn Waugh

C – Graham Greene

D – JK Rowling

334) Which novelist wrote 'Oliver Twist' and 'Great Expectations'?

A – Robert Louise Stevenson

B – Charles Dickens

C – Graham Greene

D – JK Rowling

335) William Wordsworth wrote what?

A – Non-fiction books

B – Poems

C – Film scripts

D – Fiction novels

336) Some of the best regarded poets are buried or remembered where in London?

A – Poets Corner

B – Poets Gardens

C – Poets Towers

D – Poets Factory

---- Leisure ----

337) **What is the word for a garden that people in the UK can rent, which is not part of their home?**

A – An alittlement

B – An air garden

C – Hydroponic garden

D – An allotment

338) **Which flower is associated with England?**

A – The daffodil

B – The shamrock

C – The thistle

D – The rose

339) **Which flower is associated with Scotland?**

A – The daffodil

B – The shamrock

C – The thistle

D – The rose

340) **Which flower is associated with Northern Ireland?**

A – The daffodil

B – The shamrock

C – The thistle

D – The rose

341) **Which flower is associated with Wales?**

A – The daffodil

B – The shamrock

C – The thistle

D – The rose

342) **What is the central shopping area of a town called?**

A – The town centre

B – Suburbs

C – The central business district

D – High street

343) True or False: Many (but not all) families eat Yorkshire pudding with roast beef, gravy, potatoes, and vegetables on Sundays.

344) True or False: Haggis is a commonly consumed snack in England.

345) In which year were films first shown publicly in the UK?
A – 1986
B – 1896
C – 1698
D – 1968

346) Which animated films were written by Nick Park?
A – James Bond
B – Wallace and Gromit
C – Carry On
D – Lady Luck

347) True or False: Recent British actors to win Oscars include Kate Winslet and Colin Firth.

348) True or False: An important part of UK character is being able to laugh at ourselves, with comedy and satire.

349) What is the British equivalent of the Oscars?
A – The BAFTA's
B – The Mercury Awards
C – The Emmy
D – The Logie Award

350) Which of the following is a popular current soap opera TV show?

A – Home and Away

B – Neighbours

C – Coronation Street

D – The Chase

351) Is it law that everybody watching television in the UK (whether on TV or a computer) must pay for a TV license?

A – Yes

B – No

352) If you watch TV without a license in the home, what is the maximum fine applicable?

A – £1M

B – £100,000

C – £15,000

D – £1,000

353) What does the money generated from the TV license fund?

A – The BBC

B – Rich shareholders

C – Government MPs

D – Free school meals

354) Which is NOT a popular social network that people in the UK use to keep in communication with each other?

A – Instagram

B – Facebook

C – Twitter

D – WeChat

355) True or False: Playing darts, pool, drinking beer, and quizzes are traditional activities that British people do at public houses, or pubs as they are more widely known.

356) What is the drinking age in the UK to buy alcohol?
A – 14
B – 16
C – 18
D – 21

357) What is the drinking age in the UK to buy alcohol when with a parent and eating a meal at the same time?
A – 14
B – 16
C – 18
D – 21

358) True or False: Dog owners must ensure their dogs are wearing a collar showing their owner's name and address when out in public.

359) True or False: Pet owners are allowed to be cruel and neglectful in some scenarios.

---- UK Places of Interest ----

360) The UK offers lots of outdoor spaces for mountain biking, mountaineering, camping, and hill walking. How many national parks are there in England, Scotland, and Wales?
A – 5
B – 15
C – 24

D – 34

361) What is the name of the popular clock at the Houses of Parliament in London?

A – Big Time

B – Big Ben

C – Big Alfie

D – Big James

362) Where is the Eden Project found?

A – Bath

B – Brighton

C – Cromwell

D – Cornwall

363) In which country is the Giant's Causeway located?

A – England

B – Scotland

C – Wales

D – Northern Ireland

364) When was the Giant's Causeway formed?

A – 50,000 years ago

B – 50 million years ago

C – 5 billion years ago

D – 500 years ago

365) Loch Lomond is the largest body of fresh water in mainland Britain, which country is it located in?

A – England

B – Scotland

C – Wales

D – Northern Ireland

LIFE IN THE UK TEST 2023

366) Snowdonia is a national park covering 823 square miles, which country is it located in?

A – England

B – Scotland

C – Wales

D – Northern Ireland

367) Who was the Tower of London built by after he was crowned King in 1066?

A – King James II

B – King Henry VII

C – William The Conqueror

D – King Henry VIII

368) Which is England's largest national park?

A – Dartmoor

B – The Lake District

C – The Peak District

D – Snowdonia

369) The Lake District is famous for what?

A – Windmills

B – Tall buildings

C – Very sunny, stunning weather

D – Lakes and mountains

4

The Government, Law, and
Your Role

---- British Democracy and The Constitution----

370) In the democratic system, who gets a say in decisions that are made?
A – Only men
B – Only women
C – Only adults
D – Every man, woman, and child

371) In the 1830s and 40s, which group campaigned for reform of voting rights?
A – The Charlatans
B – The Chartists
C – The Arrows
D – The Clubs

372) True or False: The British Constitution has been written down in a single document.

373) True or False: The British Constitution contains laws, conventions as well as institutions responsible for leading the country.

374) Who is the current head of the Monarchy for the UK and other countries in the Commonwealth?
A – Queen Camilla
B – Queen Elizabeth II
C – King Andrew
D – King Charles III

375) Under a constitutional monarchy, does the King or Queen decide government policy?
A – No
B – Yes
C – No, but he/she does communicate with and support the government
D – Yes, but only on weekends

376) Who is the current heir to the throne?
A – Prince Harry
B – Queen Camilla
C – Prince Andrew
D – Prince William

377) What is the current national anthem of the UK?
A – God Save the King
B – God Save the Queen
C – England is my Country
D – The Three Lions

378) In which year did Queen Elizabeth II celebrate 70 years on the throne?
A – 2011

B – 2016

C – 2021

D – 2022

379) True or False: New citizens must affirm loyalty to the King or Queen as part of the citizenship ceremony.

380) What is the system of government defined as in the UK?

A – Socialism

B – Nationalism

C – Monarch rule

D – Parliamentary democracy

381) What are voters' regions called?

A – Districts

B – Constituencies

C – Clans

D – Kingdoms

382) If two parties join due to a lack of majority, what is this type of government called? (This most recently happened in 2010 with the Conservatives and Liberal Democrats.)

A – A joining

B – A formation

C – A coalition

D – A combination

383) Why is the House of Commons thought to be more important than the House of Lords?

A – Because the royalty prefers it

B – Because its members are elected

C – Because there are more members

D – Because the members are paid a salary

384) True or False: At present, do people who inherit the title of Lord automatically get to attend the House of Lords?

385) True or False: The House of Commons actually has the strength to overpower the House of Lords.

386) Who chairs the debates in the House of Commons?
A – The Speaker
B – The Spokesperson
C – The Deputy Prime Minister
D – The Prime Minister

387) The speaker does not represent a political party even though he/she is a member of Parliament. How is the Speaker chosen?
A – By the public
B – By online voting
C – By secret MP ballot
D – By the King or Queen

388) What does the Speaker of the House do?
A – Speaks his/her opinion on political matters and economics
B – Ensures the debate rules are followed
C – Take notes
D – Speaks on the King/Queen's behalf

389) How often is a general election held in the British Isles?
A – At least every 4 years
B – At least every 5 years
C – At least every 6 years
D – At least every 7 years

390) If a Prime Minister resigns during his or her reign, which election takes place?
A – A coalition
B – A formation
C – A general election
D – A by-election

391) Which British politician served as Prime Minister of the United Kingdom after previously serving as Leader of the Conservative Party, Foreign Secretary, and Mayor of London?
A – Boris Johnson
B – Theresa May
C – Rishi Sunak
D – Liz Truss

---- The Government ----

392) What is the address of the Prime Minister?
A – 10 Royal Road
B – 10 Downing Street
C – 14 Royal Road
D – 14 Downing Street

393) Who appoints the Cabinet?
A – The Prime Minister
B – The Monarchy
C – The public
D – The Speaker

394) What is the Chancellor of the Exchequer responsible for?
A – The Bank of England

B – The economy

C – Schools

D – Policing

395) What is the opposition?

A – The Enemy

B – Russia

C – France

D – The second largest party in the House of Commons

396) The leader of the opposition also appoints Ministers, what are they called?

A – Fake Ministers

B – Future Ministers

C – Shadow Ministers

D – Untapped Ministers

397) True or False: Anyone over 18 can stand for an election, even if they are not representing one of the major political parties.

398) People not representing a major party but standing in the election are called what:

A – Individualists

B – Independents

C – Separatists

D – Outsiders

399) Which of these is not a major political party in the UK?

A – Liberal Democrats

B – Labour

C – Conservative

D – Scottish Greens

400) What do pressure or lobby groups do?

A – Try to become MPs

B – Try to influence policy

C – Try to make profit

D – Try to start civil wars

401) True or False: Civil Servants are members of the party which is leading at the time.

402) What do civil servants not do?

A – Deliver public services

B – Work for ministers

C – Implement government policies

D – Work for free

403) True or False: Local authorities (governments) are funded by the main government and by local taxes.

404) How many local authorities does London have?

A – 28

B – 29

C – 34

D – 33

405) In which month do most local authority elections take place?

A – May

B – June

406) In which year was power devolved to give people in Wales, Scotland, and Northern Ireland more power to govern the matters which directly affect them?

A – 1977

B – 1997

C – 1991

D – 2000

407) What is the more accurate word for the Welsh assembly?
A – The Senedd
B – The Glycoled
C – The Senatt
D – None of the above

408) True or False: The Senedd makes laws in 21 areas across education, housing, economics, and more. The Senedd can also pass laws on these topics without approval from the UK Parliament.

409) The Scottish Parliament was created in 1999. In which city can you find it?
A – Aberdeen
B – Fife
C – Glasgow
D – Edinburgh

410) True or False: The Scottish Parliament members are also elected by proportional representation, they can vote on every matter.

411) When was the Northern Ireland Assembly created?
A – After the Belfast Agreement in 1998
B – 1922
C – 1978
D – 1969

412) There are MLAs (Member of the Legislative Assembly) in Northern Ireland, which of the following do they NOT make decisions on?

A – Education

B – Agriculture

C – The Northern Ireland football squad

D – The environment

413) In which of the following countries has the UK previously used its power to suspend devolved assemblies?

A – Scotland

B – Northern Ireland

C – Wales

D – Australia

414) Parliamentary decisions are recorded in which official reports?

A – Farmyard

B – Lanyard

C – Hansard

D – Mansard

415) True or False: The UK has a free press meaning that newspapers are free from governmental control.

416) True or False: Media coverage must not be biased.

417) If you are allowed to vote, must you be on what is called the electoral

register?

A – No

B – Yes

418) Electoral registration is sent out every September or October, what must you include when you send it back?

A – Names of eligible voters in the household

B – Political party that everybody in the household expects to vote for

C – A voting fee

D – Your tax number

419) Where does voting take place when in the UK?

A – Via Facebook

B – Via a letter to Parliament

C – At the Town Hall

D – At polling stations

420) What time are polling stations open on Election Day?

A – 7am to 10pm

B – 8am to 10pm

C – 8am to 6pm

D – 7am to midnight

421) True or False: You can view the list of voters at the local authority/some libraries.

422) True or False: Everybody has the right to try and convince you to vote for a specific candidate.

423) If you cannot attend the polling station (for example when on holiday), what should you do?

A – Give up on voting

B – Get your friend to vote for you

C – Get a family member to vote for you

D – Send a postal vote

424) Which of the following CAN stand for office?

A – Civil servants

B – Criminals

C – Army personnel

D – Over 18's in the UK

425) True or False: You can get free tickets to watch debates in the UK Parliament.

426) True or False: Voting in the UK is compulsory for citizens between 18 and 65 years old.

---- The UK/ International Institutions ----

427) What is the current goal of the Commonwealth?
A – To work toward common goals and help each other
B – To reform the British Empire
C – To destroy the British Empire
D – To recruit new countries

428) King Charles III is the head of the Commonwealth, which currently has how many states?
A – 54
B – 22
C – 56
D – 100

429) How much power does the Commonwealth have over its members?
A – None
B – None, but it can stop membership
C – Sufficient power to oversee the affairs of its members
D – Absolute power

430) Which of these is not a core value of the Commonwealth?
A – Democracy
B – Law

C – Freedom

D – Good government

431) True or False: Singapore is a member of the Commonwealth.

432) True or False: Switzerland is a member of the Commonwealth.

433) Which of these is not an international organisation of which the UK is a
member?
A – NATO
B – The Council of Europe
C – The UN
D – The EU

434) The Council of Europe is most well-known for defending what?
A – European borders
B – Human rights
C – Tax laws
D – The British Royalty

---- Respecting the Law ----

435) True or False: Every person in the UK receives equal treatment under the law, including non-citizens.

436) True or False: Criminal law is different from civil law as it only relates to crimes, rather than settling disputes.

437) Which of the following are NOT examples of illegal crimes?
A – Buying alcohol for somebody under 18

B – Making jokes about the government

C – Owing unpaid debt/money

D – Drinking alcohol in public

438) Which of these is NOT an example of civil law?

A – Housing Law

B – Selling or buying drugs

C – Consumer rights

D – Employment Law

439) The three general duties of the police are to protect life/ property, keep the peace, and prevent/detect crime. Which of the following is NOT true?

A – The police are independent of the government

B – If police officers are corrupt or misuse their authority they are severely punished.

C – The police protect everyone, no matter their background or where they live

D – The police in the UK are also commonly known as the FBI

440) Who sets the local police budget?

A – The Prime Minister

B – The Monarch

C – The Chief Constable

D – The Police and Crime Commissioners (PCCs)

441) True or False: The police themselves must also obey the law.

442) True or False: Police Community Support Officers (PCSOs) have the power to arrest someone.

443) The UK faces terrorist threats, where are these supposedly from?

A – Al Qaida and Northern Ireland related groups

B – Denmark and Switzerland

C – The Isle of Man

D – Argentina

444) The Judiciary refers to what?

A – A park in London

B – Judges

---- The Role of Courts ----

445) True or False: The Government must change the law if the Judiciary deem they have done something illegal.

446) When a public body is thought to have not respected somebody's rights, what are they usually ordered to do?

A – Pay compensation/change practises

B – Go to prison

C – Pay more taxes in the future

D – Fire their leader

447) In England, Wales, and Northern Ireland, minor criminal cases are usually dealt with at which court?

A – Justice of the Peace Court

B – Magistrates Court

C – Sherriff Court

D – Crown Courts

448) In Scotland, the same minor criminal cases are dealt with at which court?

A – Justice of the Peace Court

B – Magistrates Court

C – Sherriff Court

D – Crown Courts

449) In England, Wales, and Northern Ireland, where are serious offences tried?

A – Justice of the Peace Court

B – Magistrates Court

C – Sherriff Court

D – Crown Courts

450) In Scotland, where are serious criminal offences tried?

A – Justice of the Peace Court

B – Magistrates Court

C – Sherriff Court

D – Crown Courts

451) True or False: Magistrates and Justice of the Peace Judges do not need legal qualifications.

452) True or False: In Northern Ireland, small crimes are also decided by unqualified and unpaid Judges.

453) In all countries in the UK, for serious cases like murder, who is also present alongside the Judges?

A – Jury

B – Sniffer dogs

C – The army

D – The High Commissioner

454) What is a jury?

A – Volunteers from the public

B – Members of the public chosen at random

LIFE IN THE UK TEST 2023

455) True or False: Jury service is optional when you are asked to do it.

456) True or False: The jury decides on the penalty given to a criminal.

457) How many members are on the jury in Scotland?
A – 10
B – 12
C – 15
D – 17

458) In England, Wales, or Northern Ireland, where would somebody ages 10 and 17 who committed a crime go to court?
A – Magistrates Court
B – Dedicated Youth Court
C – A Juvenile Court
D – Crown Courts

459) Which type of judge oversees cases at a Youth Court?
A – Specially trained Magistrates or a District Judge
B – Unpaid Magistrates
C – Junior Judges
D – Senior Judges

460) If somebody in England, Wales, or Northern Ireland between ages 10 and 17 commits a serious crime, which court would they go to?
A – Crown Court
B – Dedicated Youth Court
C – Magistrates Court
D – A Juvenile Court

461) What is not allowed to be published about dealings in the court for people ages 10 and 17?
A – Names and photographs
B – Details about the crime

462) Which court deals with civil disputes in England, Wales, and Northern Ireland?
A – The Magistrates Court
B – The Crown Court
C – The Sheriff Court
D – The County Courts

463) Which of these matters would not be dealt with at a county court?
A – Contractual arguments
B – Armed robbery
C – Family arguments
D – Owing personal debts

464) For more serious civil matters, like when large amounts of money are being claimed as compensation – where could these be dealt with in England, Wales, and Northern Ireland?
A – The High Court
B – Magistrates Court
C – County Court
D – The Court of Session

465) For more serious civil matters, like when large amounts of money are being claimed as compensation, where could these be dealt with in Scotland?
A – The High Court
B – Magistrates Court
C – County Court

D – The Court of Session, which is in Edinburgh

466) True or False: The small claims procedure is for helping people settle minor disputes for amounts of money below £10,000 in England/Wales or below £3,000 in Scotland and Northern Ireland.

467) True or False: Solicitors are lawyers who can represent their clients.

---- Fundamental Principles ----

468) When did the UK sign the European Human Rights Convention?
A – 1940
B – 1950
C – 1960
D – 1970

469) Which of these is not part of the European Convention of Human Rights?
A – Freedom of speech
B – Driving your car at any speed
C – Prohibition of slavery / forced labour
D – Right to liberty and security

470) True or False: The UK is a place of equal opportunity for all.

471) True or False: Violence and brutality in the home is a serious offence.

472) Which of the following is acceptable in the UK?

A – Forced marriage

B – Arranged marriage

C – Underage marriage

D – Marriage in lieu of outstanding debts

473) If anybody is trying to force a marriage, they can go to jail for how long?

A – 2 years

B – 6 years

C – 10 years

D – 10 days

---- Our Taxation----

474) What is the UK's stance on taxation?

A – Taxation is beneficial to society

B – Taxation is theft

C – Taxation is optional

D – Taxation is detrimental to society

475) People in the UK pay income tax from their employment, self-employment and income from some investments. What does this money help fund?

A – Roads, schools, the army, and more

B – The Prime Minister's private lunch expenses

C – Former colonies

D – War reparations

476) True or False: Employed people pay tax via PAYE (Pay as you earn).

477) True or False: Self-employed people also pay taxes via PAYE.

478) True or False: Self-employed individuals are allowed to have their friends pay
their tax liabilities on their behalf?

479) What other tax must all working people in the UK contribute?
A – Building Insurance
B – Nature Tax
C – Child Tax
D – National Insurance

480) What does National Insurance fund?
A – The National Trust
B – State benefits
C – Food providers
D – Coffee plantations

481) At what age do you receive a National Insurance number?
A – 14
B – 16
C – 18
D – 20

---- UK Driving ----

482) What is the age at which you can learn to drive?
A – 17
B – 18
C – 19
D – 21

483) True or False: Moped drivers can begin to learn at age 16.

484) True or False: The driving test in the UK includes only a theoretical test.

485) What must newly qualified drivers in Northern Ireland display?

A – A 'R' plate

B – A 'P' plate

C – Nothing

D – A "RP" plate

486) For how long can you use a driving license from another country in the UK?

A – 3 months

B – 6 months

C – 12 months

D – 2 years

487) What should you do if your vehicle is not being used?

A – Pay a reduced tax

B – Pay more tax

C – Nothing

D – Make a SORN (an off-road-notice)

488) Not having car insurance is a serious offence. If your vehicle is more than three years old, what must you do with your car every year?

A – Take it out of the country

B – Sell it for a new one

C – Trade it for an electric one

D – Take it for a MOT Test

---- Your Role in the Community ----

489) When you move to a new house or apartment, what is it custom to do?
A – Play loud music and leave rubbish on the street
B – Get to know your neighbours

490) Volunteering at schools is a good way to demonstrate what?
A – That you are a good citizen
B – That you are educated
C – You have money and success
D – You are British

491) Which of the following ways is NOT a standard way to help at a school?
A – Helping students to read
B – Helping at a book sale or on school trips, or bringing food
C – Joining a parent-teacher association or becoming a school governor
D – Telling others in the community to join the same school

492) How should you approach becoming a school governor?
A – Write a letter to the local minister
B – Call the school
C – Apply online
D – Demand that you are eligible to become governor

493) True or False: You can join a political party and hand out leaflets for them – this is called canvassing.

494) True or False: There are also possibilities to help at local youth projects, universities, housing groups, museums, and more.

495) True or False: It is possible to volunteer with the police.

496) True or False: Giving blood takes less than an hour and can save countless lives of your fellow citizens.

497) Which of these is NOT a tangible benefit you will get from volunteering?
A – Practising your English skills
B – Improving your CV (curriculum vitae)
C – Improving your community
D – Earning money

498) Which of these is not an example of volunteering?
A – Working at a pet rescue place
B – Delivering takeaway for Uber Eats
C – Mentoring/coaching young people
D – Joining a litter pick-up

499) True or False: There are also many charities you can volunteer with and donate to, for example, you can volunteer for Oxfam at Summer Music Festivals and receive a free ticket.

500) True or False: People aged 18 and under are also allowed to volunteer.

That brings us to the end of the practise questions. I hope that you enjoyed the format of this book – and that you also learned a lot about the UK along the way.

If you need to, re-read this book until you are confident in answering at least 90% of the questions as this will give you the best chance of success on the day of your examination.

If you found this book beneficial, please leave us a positive review on Amazon. Thank you and good luck – we look forward to having you as an honorary citizen or permanent resident in the UK.

In the next chapter will follow the answers, followed by handy lists of all the Monarchs, as well as some important sports and cultural personalities for you to remember.

5

Answers

---- Early Britain ----

1) The first people to live in Britain were hunter-gathers, who lived in which age?
B – The Stone Age

2) How did people in Britain get to the European continent during the Stone Age?
C – By a land bridge
Note: Britain was connected to the European continent by a land bridge for much of the Stone Age, allowing people to come and go.

3) When did Britain become permanently separated from the continent of Europe?
C – 10,000 years ago

4) Some of the first farmers arrived in Britain 6,000 years ago, which of the following did they build?
D – Stonehenge

5) Which county is the Stonehenge monument located in?
D – Wiltshire

6) **Which country in the British Isles can you find the island, Orkney?**

B – Scotland

Note: Orkney is one of the best-preserved prehistoric villages in Europe and offers archaeologists and visitors a glimpse into how people lived during the Stone Age.

7) **True or False: The Bronze Age was followed by the Iron Age.**

Answer – True

8) **When roughly was the Bronze Age?**

A – 4,000 years ago

9) **In which period did people begin to create Britain's first coins and trading economy?**

A – The Iron Age

10) **Who led the failed Roman invasion of Britain in 55 BC (before Christ)?**

B – Julius Caesar

11) **The Romans later succeeded in occupying most of Britain, which year did this happen?**

B – 43 AD

12) **The Statue of Boudicca is found where in London?**

D – On Westminster Bridge

Note: Queen Boudicca was a tribal leader from a region in the east of England who led a failed uprising against the Romans.

13) **True or False: Hadrian's Wall protected the area that we now call Scotland from ever being conquered by the Romans.**

Answer – False, the wall was actually built by the Romans, named after Emperor Hadrian, as a frontier to their empire and to provide protection from the north.

14) During the 400 years the Romans remained in Britain, what did they NOT create?
A – English food

15) Did the Romans ever return after leaving the British Isles? Yes or No?
A – No

16) When the Anglo-Saxon Kingdoms were established around 600 AD, which parts of Britain remained mostly free of Anglo-Saxon rule?
A – Wales and Scotland

17) True or False: The languages of the Jutes, Angles, and Saxons (who invaded Britain) formed the basis of the modern English language.
Answer – True

18) Who was the most famous Christian missionary to influence the Anglo-Saxons?
A – St. Patrick, who became the Patron Saint of Ireland

19) Who spread Christianity in the south of Britain?
B – St. Augustine
Note: St Augustine led missionaries from Rome and became the first Archbishop of Canterbury.

20) Where did the Vikings come from?
D – Denmark, Norway, and Sweden

21) When did the Vikings first raid Britain for goods and slaves?
B – 789 AD

22) True or False: The Vikings defeated the Anglo-Saxons.
Answer – False, the Anglo-Saxons defeated the Vikings under King Alfred the Great

23) Some of the Vikings stayed in Britain in an area called Danelaw in the northeast of England. Which towns can be found there now?
A – Grimsby and Scunthorpe
Note that New Danelaw does not exist! Grimsby and Scunthorpe, meanwhile, originate from Viking languages.

24) The Anglo-Saxons ruled England, except for a short time where Danish Kings ruled. What was the name of the first of these Kings?
A – Cnut

25) In which year did the Battle of Hastings take place?
D – 1066

26) Which King was killed in the Battle of Hastings, by William the Duke of Normandy?
A – Harold

27) King William became known as:
C – William the Conqueror

28) The Battle of Hastings is commemorated by which piece of art?
B – The Bayeux Tapestry
Note: This famous tapestry can still be seen today in France.

29) True or False: The Norman Conquest was the most recent successful foreign invasion of England.

Answer – True

30) True or False: The Normans also conquered Wales.

Answer – True, however the Welsh slowly won territory back

31) True or False: The Normans conquered Scotland.

Answer – False, although the Normans did reclaim some land on the border of England and Scotland

32) King William created a list of who owned all the land and the animals that people owned in England. What was this list called?

A – Domesday Book

---- The Middle Ages ----

33) Which period of history does the following section on the Middle Ages focus on?

B – After the Norman Conquest

34) In which year did King Edward I of England introduce the state of Rhuddlan, which annexed Wales to the Crown of England?

D – 1284

35) In which country in Britain can you find the castles of Caernarvon and Conwy?

B – Wales

Note that Wales also has the most castles in Britain, with well over 500 of them!

36) **True or False: The last of the Welsh rebellions were defeated in the 16th Century.**

Answer – False, the last rebellions were in the 15th Century, and after this, English laws and language were introduced to Wales

37) **Scotland fought England and again was not conquered in the Battle of Bannockburn in 1314. Who was the battle led by on the Scotland side?**

C – Robert the Bruce

38) **Around the year 1200, the English ruled an area then known as Pale. Which city is it now known as?**

D – Dublin

39) **How long did the Hundred Years' War last?**

C – 116 years

40) **Who was involved in the Hundred Years' War?**

B – England and France

41) **In which war did King Henry V's English army heavily defeat the French army?**

A – The Battle of Agincourt

42) **True or False: The English mostly left France in the 1450s.**

Answer – True

43) **The system of Kings giving land to Lords is called what?**

D – Feudalism

44) **In the North of Scotland, a different system was operated, where land was owned by members of the what?**

B – Clans

45) What was the Black Death?
A – A form of plague

46) How much of the English, Scottish, and Welsh population died during the plague?
C – Around 30%

47) True or False: The plague led to excess labour and falling wages.
Answer – False, in fact, it led to labour shortages and larger wage demands

48) True or False: Before 1215 the King's power was absolute, it was only after 1215 that the King (John) was forced by his noblemen to agree to some of their requests.
Answer – True

49) The result of this limited power led to which Charter of Rights Agreement?
B – Magna Carta
Note: 'Manga Carta' means Great Charter in Latin, a language used by the Romans.

50) What was the function of the Magna Carta?
A – To restrict the rights of the King to collect taxes or change laws

51) As more people joined Parliament, two separate houses were created. What were these houses called and are still called today?
B – The House of Lords and the House of Commons

52) True or False: Scotland also had two houses in their Parliament.

Answer – False, they had three houses, the Lords, the Commons, and the Clergy

53) What was introduced in the legal system by the Judges in England at this time?

D – Common Law

Note: Common Law evolves by a process of precedence where laws are based on previous decisions and tradition.

54) True or False: Scotland also applied Common Law during this period.

Answer – False, laws were instead codified, meaning they were written down, and therefore more rigid than Common Law

55) At this point in time in the Middle Ages (after the Norman Conquest in the 1200s), what language did the King and his people speak?

A – French

56) What language did the peasants speak at this same time?

C – Anglo-Saxon (also known as 'Old English')

57) True or False: Eventually, these languages merged to become what we know as English, with some Anglo-Saxon words and other words from French.

Answer – True

58) True or False: By 1400, official papers in the Parliament were being written in the English language.

Answer – True

59) Geoffrey Chaucer's series of poems about a pilgrimage is called what?

B – The Canterbury Tales

60) Who was the first person to print books in England using a printing press?

A – William Caxton

61) During this time (around the 1400s) in Scotland, which language was mostly spoken?

B – Gaelic

62) John Barber, a poet in Scotland wrote 'The Bruce' about which battle?

A – The Battle of Bannockburn

63) During the Middle Ages, which kind of buildings were built?

D – Castles and cathedrals

64) True or False: Windsor Castle and Edinburgh Castle are no longer in use.

Answer – False, these two castles are still in use today

65) During the Middle Ages, England was heavily involved in trading with other countries. Which of the following was a famous export from England?

C – Wool

66) Foreigners also came from continental Europe to England for work. Where did the weavers come from?

A – France

67) Foreigners also came from Europe to England for work. Where did the engineers come from?

B – Germany

68) Where did the glass makers come from?
D – Italy

69) Where did the canal builders come from?
C – Holland

70) In the year 1455, which civil war began to decide the King of England?
D – The Wars of the Roses

71) True or False: The Wars of the Roses was fought between the House of Commons and the House of Lords.
Answer – False, the wars were fought between the House of Lancaster and The House of York

72) What is the symbol of the House of Lancaster?
A – A red rose

73) What is the symbol of the House of York?
B – A white rose

74) The end of the Wars of the Roses was in which year, signified by the Battle of Bosworth Field?
D – 1485

75) True or False: King Richard III was killed in battle at Bosworth Field.
Answer – True

76) Who succeeded King Richard III after his death?
A – King Henry VII

77) After King Henry VII married Elizabeth of York (which united the two families), what was the new symbol of the House of Tudor?

D – A red rose with a white rose inside

---- The Tudors and Stuarts ----

78) What did King Henry VII do after his victory in the Wars of the Roses?

C – Reduced the power of the nobles

79) When Henry VII died, his son (Henry VIII) continued the reign of power, but what was Henry VIII most famous for?

A – Leaving the church of Rome and having six wives

80) King Henry VIII died of which cause?

B – Obesity and physical decline

81) Who was the first wife of Henry VIII?

D – Catherine of Aragon

82) Why did Henry decide to annul (declare the marriage had no legal existence) his first wife Catherine of Aragon, without the approval of the Pope?

B – To find another wife who could give him a son and be heir to the throne

83) True or False: Henry VIII's second wife (Anne Boleyn) was executed at the Tower of London as she was said to have taken lovers.

Answer – True

84) True or False: Henry VIII's third wife (Jane Seymour) gave Henry the heir to the throne that he was looking for.

Answer – True, but she died shortly after

85) Why did Henry VIII marry his fourth wife (Anne of Cleves)?

D – For political reasons

86) What was the fate of Henry VIII's wife (Catherine Howard)?

B – She was executed for taking lovers

87) The final wife of Henry VIII was a widow named Catherine Parr. Who died first, her or King Henry VIII?

B – King Henry VIII

88) When the Pope did not allow King Henry VIII to divorce his first wife, what did Henry do?

A – He established the Church of England

89) As England and the rest of Europe moved from Roman Catholic to the Church of England, what was this transition called?

D – The Reformation

90) True or False: The Protestants formed their own churches where they did not pray to saints or shrines.

Answer – True

91) True or False: Protestant culture lost strength in England, Wales, and Scotland during the 16th Century.

Answer – False, it actually gained strength

92) Over in Ireland, English attempts to impose Protestant rule led to violent rebellion by which Irish group?

B – The Chieftains

93) What did Henry VIII accomplish during his time as King?
A – He united Wales with England

94) Who was King Henry VIII succeeded by after his death?
C – King Edward VI

95) At what age did King Edward VI die?
A – 15

96) Which book was written during Edward VI's rule in Britain?
B – The Book of Common Prayer

97) True or False: After King Edward VI's death, his half-sister Mary took the throne.
Answer – True

98) True or False: Queen Mary was succeeded by Elizabeth, the youngest offspring of Henry VIII and his second wife.
Answer – True

99) What was Queen Elizabeth I's religious preference?
B – Protestant
Note: Queen Elizabeth re-established the Church of England as the official Church in England.

100) How did Queen Elizabeth I allow for religious harmony in England?
A – She appreciated the views of both the Catholics and the Protestants
B – She did not ask about people's real beliefs
Answer – Both

101) Why was Elizabeth I such a popular monarch?

D – She defeated the Spanish Armada (a fleet of ships) in 1588

102) Over in Scotland, the mostly Protestant Parliament also abolished the Pope's authority and Roman Catholic services were made illegal by law. Who was the Queen of Scotland at this time?

A – Mary Stuart, now also known as 'Mary, Queen of Scots'

Note: Born a Catholic and growing up in France, Queen Mary was only a week old when her father died and she became Queen.

103) True or False: After returning from France to Scotland, Mary was suspected to be involved in the murder of her husband. She then fled to England, giving the throne to her Protestant son, James VI of Scotland.

Answer – True

104) What was the fate of Mary when she arrived in England?

B – She was held prisoner for 20 years, and later executed by Queen Elizabeth I

105) The Elizabethan era was a time of what in England?

B – Pride of being English

106) Who was Sir Francis Drake?

B – A founder of England's naval tradition

107) What was the name of the ship Sir Francis Drake sailed around the world?

D – The Golden Hind

108) During Elizabeth I's reign, which region did English settlers begin to colonise?

A – Eastern coast of America

109) The Elizabethan era is also fondly recollected for poetry. Which of the following is a famous English poet and playwriter?
C – William Shakespeare

110) Where was William Shakespeare born?
C – Stratford-upon-Avon

111) Which of the following is not a poem or play written by William Shakespeare?
A – Roses

112) Shakespeare was one of the first poets to do what?
C – Include ordinary English men and women

113) William Shakespeare was born in 1564 and died in what year?
A – 1616

114) True or False: Shakespeare's plays and poems are still studied today across many schools in England.
Answer – True

115) In which London Theatre is a modern take of Shakespeare's plays still performed today?
A – The Globe Theatre

116) True or False: When Queen Elizabeth I died, Elizabeth II took the throne.
False – Elizabeth I did not have children, so in 1603 James VI of Scotland became King James I of England, Wales, and Ireland. At this point, Scotland was its own country.

117) What was the main achievement or notable production of King James during his time in power?

D – Creation of the King James Bible

Note: The King James Bible is a new translation of the Bible into English and continues to be used in many Protestant churches today.

118) True or False: Protestant settlements during this time in Ireland were known as plantations.

Answer – True

119) King James I's son was called what name?

A – Charles I

120) Why did the Scottish army rebel against Charles I?

B – Because he attempted to introduce a prayer book to the Presbyterian Church

121) After the Civil War began in 1642, the country split into which two sets of people – The Cavaliers and the Roundheads. Who did the Cavaliers support?

B – The Kings

122) Charles I's army was defeated in 1646 in which battle(s)?

C – The Battle of Marston Moor and Battle of Naseby

123) Charles I was held by the Parliament's army and executed in which year?

B – 1649

124) After the execution, England became a republic. What was it called?

D – The Commonwealth

125) One of the generals in the army at this time, Oliver Cromwell, became famed for what during his successful power grab in the English Parliament?

D – For being so violent

126) When Charles II's Scottish army attacked England, Cromwell defeated them. Where did Charles II famously hide during his escape from Worcester?

A – Inside a tree

127) After his success, Cromwell was named leader of the republic and was called Lord Protector. Who succeeded him after his death in 1658?

A – His son, Richard

128) Sadly, Richard was not such a great leader as Oliver Cromwell and people demanded that a King be restored. Who returned from Europe (Holland) and was crowned King of England, Wales, Scotland, and Ireland in 1660?

A – Charles II

129) Was this the only known period of time that England was a republic?

A – Yes

130) True or False: This time, Charles II would cooperate with Parliament and the Church of England again became the official Church.

Answer – True

131) During Charles II's reign, which major event occurred in 1666?

D – The Great Fire of London

132) Which landmark in London was famously rebuilt after this great fire?

C – St. Paul's Cathedral

133) In 1679, which important act was introduced?

B – The Habeas Corpus

134) Charles II was also interested in science and helped to create the Royal Society. Which well-known individual originated from that society?

B – Isaac Newton

135) What scientific principle did Isaac Newton famously discover and demonstrate?

C – Gravity

136) Isaac Newton studied at which university?

A – Cambridge University

137) In 1685, Charles II (who had no children) died. Who was given the throne?

A – His brother, James

138) Which religion did King James II favour?

B – Roman Catholic

139) Why did people stop worrying that England would become a Catholic country under James II?

B – Because his daughters (heirs) were Protestant

140) True or False: The Glorious Revolution was "glorious" because there was no fighting.

Answer – True

141) What did the Glorious Revolution achieve?

B – It meant there was no threat of the Monarchy having total control

142) True or False: After William of Orange invaded England during the Glorious Revolution, James fled to France. Later he wanted to regain the throne, so he attacked Ireland with the help of a French army and won the battle of Boyne in 1960.

Answer – False, while James did flee to France and he did return to attack Ireland, he lost the Battle of Boyne. King William III re-conquered Ireland and James again fled back to France. The Battle of Boyne is still celebrated in Northern Ireland to this day.

143) James still had some supporters in Scotland and even in England. What did his supporters become known as?

C – The Jacobites

---- A Global Power ----

144) At the coronation of William and Mary, which bill was written in 1689?

A – The Bill of Rights

145) What did the Bill of Rights achieve?

A – Further limits to the King's power

146) True or False: The Parliament decided that each new King or Queen must be
Catholic.

Answer – False, the new King or Queen had to be a Protestant

147) The bill concluded that a new parliament had to be elected every three years, which later changed to every seven years. How many years must a parliament be re-elected today?

B – 5

148) These changes (as well as navy and army funding) meant that the Monarch required ministers to vote in the House of Commons and the House of Lords. Which were the two main groups in Parliament at this time?

D – The Whigs and the Tories

149) True or False: The Whigs are now referred to as the Conservative Party.

Answer – False, the Tories are today officially called the Conservative Party

150) This was a new time, a time of party politics. What else was also new at this time?

D – Freedom of the press

151) Which year was the freedom of the press introduced, where newspapers no longer needed a license to operate and publish their news?

C – 1695

152) True or False: After the Glorious Revolution, the British Isles was called a 'constitutional monarchy', where the King or Queen was still important but couldn't pass new laws if Parliament didn't agree.

Answer – True

153) True or False: This was now a time of democracy where anybody could vote on laws and bills in Parliament.

Answer – False, only a small number of wealthy landowners had the power to vote, and women could still not participate. Constituencies were split into what we called pocket boroughs and rotten boroughs.

154) The population in Britain increased between 1650 and 1720, where did refugees arrive from?
A – Jerusalem and France (The Jews and Huguenots)

155) Who was the successor of William III of England and William II of Scotland?
B – Queen Anne, who had no children of her own

156) Since Queen Anne had no airs to the throne in England, Wales, Scotland, and Ireland, which act was created in 1707?
D – The Acts of Union (which created the United Kingdom of Great Britain, meaning Scotland was no longer an independent land)

157) Queen Anne died in 1714, who did Parliament choose to be the next King?
A – A German, George I

158) Why was the first Prime Minister (Sir Robert Walpole) established in 1721?
C – Because George I did not speak good English

159) Until which year did the first Prime Minister control the United Kingdom?
C – 1742

160) Which rebellion occurred in 1745?
D – The Rebellion of the Scottish Clans

161) True or False: Charles Edward Stuart (otherwise called Bonnie Prince Charlie) lost the Battle of Culloden against George II (George I's son) in 1746 during the Rebellion of the Clans.

Answer – True

162) True or False: The clans became landlords and the chieftains became their paying tenants.

Answer – False, the clans had to pay rent for the land they used to the chieftains as the chieftains had the English King's favour

163) During the 'Highland Clearances', small farms or crofts were destroyed by landlords to make way for what?

A – Fields of sheep and cows

164) Who was Robert Burns?

D – A famous Scottish poet

165) The Enlightenment happened during the 18th Century. What did this involve?

A – People became interested in politics, philosophy, and science

166) Which idea from the Enlightenment era is still valid in today's day and age?

A – The idea that everyone should be entitled to their own religious or political view

167) Before the 18th Century, agriculture was the biggest source of employment in Britain. Which of the following became the biggest source of employment during the 18th and 19th Century?

D – Industrials

168) True or False: Britain was the first country to industrialise, or to use machinery and steam power on a large scale.

Answer – True

169) True or False: Steel production led to a huge rise in ships and railway building and the manufacturing industry became the main source of jobs in Britain.
Answer – True

170) What was Richard Arkwright known for?
B – His carding machine and efficiency in running factories

171) How were the working conditions during the Industrial Revolution?
B – Very poor

172) During these years, Britain also colonised many peoples in Canada, India, Africa, and other regions. Which countries did Britain import textiles, tea, and spices from?
B – India and Indonesia

173) Who mapped the coast of Australia?
A – James Cook

174) What did Sake Dean Mahomet open in London in 1810?
B – The first curry house

175) True or False: At this time, the slave trade was legal in Britain.
Answer – False, it was illegal but still happened overseas with Britain playing a large role in it

176) True or False: In the late 1700s, the Quakers opposed the slave trade and the terrible living conditions that the slaves were put under. This, as well as the abolitionists, helped to free the slaves

and by 1807 it was illegal to trade slaves in British ships and British ports.

Answer – True

177) In which year was the Emancipation Act (which abolished slavery throughout the British Empire) established?

D – 1833

178) Some of the original British families colonised North America because they wanted religious freedom and believed in liberty. Why did they begin to feel frustrated by the British Government?

C – When the government tried to tax them

179) Fighting broke out as the colonialists felt there should be 'no taxation without representation', thus, in 1776 how many colonies declared their independence?

A – 13

180) The colonists eventually defeated the British Army and the colonies became recognised as independent in 1783. Where were these 13 colonies located?

A – The east coast of America (now New York, Maryland, etc.)

181) During the 1700s, Britain fought many wars with which country?

D – France

182) True or False: During the French Revolution, the British defeated French and Spanish ships therefore winning the Battle of Trafalgar in 1805, with Nelson's Column in Trafalgar Square a tribute to the then leader of the British Navy.

Answer – True

183) True or False: The Duke of Wellington was killed in battle by the French Emperor Napoleon in 1815.

Answer – False, Napoleon was defeated by the Duke of Wellington and the Iron Duke (a nickname earned for his hard-line discipline and rule as a politician) went on to become Prime Minister of Great Britain. This victorious battle also ended the war with France.

184) Which symbol recognises the union of the United Kingdom of Great Britain and Ireland?

B – The Union Jack

185) Why are there no aspects of the Welsh flag appearing on the Union Jack?

B – Wales was already united with England when the first Union flag was designed in 1606 and was no longer a separate principality

186) Who was made Queen in 1837 at the age of just 18?

A – Queen Victoria

187) Victoria was Queen for almost 64 years. This period was a time of increasing power and financial opulence known as:

C – The Victorian Age

188) During Victoria's rule, the British Empire expanded to have a population of roughly how many people?

B – 400 million

189) True or False: Working conditions and trading laws improved during the 1800s, including women's and children's working hours, which were limited to 10 hours per day.

Answer – True

190) What is Isambard Kingdom Brunel famously known for?

A – Constructing the Great Western Railway

191) During the 19th Century, Britain was the leader of the world when it came to the iron and coal industries. Which industry did it also become a leader in at this time?

D – Financial services including banking and investing

192) Who were Britain's allies during the Crimean War from 1853 to 1856?

B – Turkey and France

Note: The Crimean War was fought by Britain, Turkey, and France against Russia and was the first war to be covered by the media via photographs and news stories.

193) What was Florence Nightingale's (1820 to 1910) occupation?

B – A nurse

Note: Born in Italy to English parents, Florence Nightingale and her fellow nurses improved hospital conditions and reduced the mortality rate while treating soldiers fighting in the Crimean War.

194) Over in Ireland, things were not so good. The majority of the population were farmers, and most depended on potatoes. Which event happened famously?

C – The Potato Famine, killing 1 million people

195) In 1832, the Reform Act gave more people the right to vote – mostly people in middle-class towns. In 1867, another reform allowed yet more people to vote, but still only property owners and not women. In 1870 and 1882, new rules gave women the right to own what?

A – Earnings and property

196) Which famous 'suffragette' was influential in giving women voting powers in 1928?

B – Emmeline Pankhurst

Note: Emmeline Pankhurst founded the Women's Franchise League in 1889, which fought for married women to vote in local elections.

197) What was the 'suffragettes' approach to achieving what they wanted?

B – Arson and hunger strikes

198) Why did people begin to question the expansion of the British Empire?

A – They thought it was a drain on national resources

B – The Boer War of 1899 to 1902 was unsuccessful

Answer – Both A and B are correct answers

199) Who wrote the poem 'If', as well as the Jungle Book story?

B – Rudyard Kipling

---- The 20th Century----

200) True or False: As a powerful nation, Britain began social programmes to support various groups such as the poor, divorced women, and unemployed, while pensions were also introduced.

Answer – True

201) Which event cut short this time of prosperity and peace in 1914?

A – World War I

202) True or False: Britain was allied with powers from around the world including Japan, Serbia, Greece, and Italy.

Answer – True

203) True or False: Around 400,000 Indians were killed during the First World War.

Answer – False, the number was around 40,000 – they were fighting for Britain across many countries across the Empire

204) The war included more than two million British casualties in total. How many British casualties were there on the first day of the Battle of the Somme in 1916?

D – 60,000

205) At 11am on which day in 1918 did World War 1 end?

B – November 11

206) What happened in 1922 in Ireland?

B – The Partition of Ireland

207) What is the violence in Ireland referred to, between those who wanted to remain with the British Government and those who wanted to continue the republic?

A – The Troubles

208) Between the First and Second World Wars, which major event happened?

C – The Great Depression

209) True or False: Car ownership doubled in Britain in the years between 1930 and 1939.

Answer – True

210) True or False: Winston Churchill became the Leader of Britain's war after Adolph Hitler invaded Poland and nearby countries in May 1940.

Answer – True

211) Is Winston Churchill an admired leader or a hated leader?

A – Admired

212) Churchill also wrote famous speeches which are still repeated today, how many times did he serve as Prime Minister?

B – 2

213) When the British evacuated France during the evacuation of Dunkirk, who helped to rescue them?

A – Volunteer boat owners and fishermen

214) Which phrase is used to describe the British spirit of pulling together during the heavy airside bombings of East London and Coventry?

B – The Blitz spirit

215) True or False: Allied forces (including the USA and others) helped to secure victory on the beaches of Normandy, France – referred to as D-Day – and defeated Germany in May 1945.

Answer – True

216) True or False: The war against Japan ended because the Japanese were tired of fighting.

Answer – False, Japan retreated because scientists in England and America had split the atom and created the atomic bomb

217) What did Alexander Fleming achieve?

C – He discovered penicillin

---- Britain Since 1945 ----

218) Britain had won the war, but at what cost? Its resources were depleted and led to what?
A – The welfare state and labour

219) Which social programme was NOT created at this time?
C – Free alcohol for all

220) What is the correct abbreviation for the North Atlantic Treaty Organisation?
A – NATO

221) Clement Attlee, Prime Minister between 1945 and 1951 was a member of which political party?
B – Labour

222) William Beverage, Liberal MP, is best known for what?
A – The Social Insurance and Allied Services Report

223) Lord Richard Austen Butler introduced which social reform in 1944?
D – Free secondary school in England and Wales

224) Why were migrants from the West Indies, India, Pakistan, and Bangladesh encouraged to come to work in the UK?
A – Because there was still a labour shortage in the UK

225) Which word was used to describe the 1960s?
C – The Swinging Sixties
Note: This decade was a period of significant social change, including relaxed laws regarding divorce and abortion, improved economic conditions, as well as major developments in British

fashion, cinema, and popular music, including the rise of The Beatles and The Rolling Stones.

226) Which of the following was NOT a feature of the 1960s?
D – Rapid globalization

227) Which 20th Century British invention was invented by John Logie Beard?
D – Television

228) Who discovered the structure of the DNA molecule in London and Cambridge?
A – Francis Crick

229) True or False: The Concorde, a supersonic aircraft that was faster than the speed of sound, was retired from service in 2003 and never resumed.
Answer – True

230) What did James Goodfellow invent?
D – The ATM

231) Which of these was not an inherent national problem in the 1970s?
D – The English football team not retaining the World Cup

232) Mary Peters was a talented:
A – Athlete

233) In which year did the UK join the European Union?
D – 1993

234) The UK decided not to use the Euro currency, what do we use instead?

D – The Great British Pound Sterling

235) The UK formally left the European Union, when?

B – January 31, 2020

236) True or False: Margaret Thatcher was the first female Prime Minister, she was a member of the Conservative Party, and the longest serving Prime Minister in the 20th Century.

Answer – True

237) True or False: Margaret Thatcher is disliked by some because she influenced the decline of traditional coal mining and ship-building industries.

Answer – True

238) In 1982, which country invaded the Falkland Islands during Margaret Thatcher's time as Prime Minister?

B – Argentina

239) Following Prime Minister Thatcher, John Major became the new Prime Minister – what did he help to restore?

A – Peace in Northern Ireland

240) Roald Dahl is most well-known for writing which books?

A – Children's stories

241) From 1997 who was elected from the Labour Party until 2007?

D – Tony Blair

242) What did Tony Blair notably introduce before he was replaced by Gordon Brown in 2007?

D – The Scottish Parliament and The Welsh Assembly

243) True or False: No political party won the majority vote in 2010.
Answer – True, it was the first time since 1974

244) True or False: On June 23, 2016, the UK voted by a margin of 51.9% to 48.1% to remain in the European Union.
Answer – False, it voted 51.9% to 48.1% in favour of leaving the European Union

---- **The UK Today** ----

245) What is the significance of Land's End and John O'Groats?
B – It represents the longest distance between two points on the mainland of the UK

246) What is the distance between Land's End and John O'Groats?
B – 1,400 kilometres

247) What is the capital city of Scotland?
B – Edinburgh

248) What is the capital city of Wales?
D – Cardiff

249) What is the only currency of the United Kingdom?
A – GBP

250) True or False: There is a 3-pence coin in the UK.
Answer – False

251) True or False: There is a 1-pound note in the UK.

Answer – False

252) True or False: There is a 5-pound coin in the UK.
Answer – False

253) True or False: There is a 50-pound note in the UK.
Answer – True

254) In different parts of the UK there are many languages and dialects, does Wales have its own language?
B – Yes, and it is taught in their schools – however many also speak English

255) Which language is also commonly spoken alongside English, in Scotland?
B – Gaelic

256) Which language is also commonly spoken alongside English, in Northern Ireland?
B – Irish Gaelic

257) What is the population of the UK as of 2022?
B – 68 million

258) What was the population of the UK in 1801?
A – 8 million

259) Which two factors have NOT led to population growth increasing during more recent years?
B – Couples being offered government money to have children
C – Longer life expectancy
Answers B and C are correct

260) True or False: the population of the UK is evenly distributed across England, Scotland, Wales, and Northern Ireland.

Answer – False, roughly 84% of the population lives in England, Scotland makes up around 8%, Wales is at 5%, and Northern Ireland less than just 3%

261) True or False: Manchester has the greatest number of inhabitants.

Answer – False, London has the most inhabitants at an estimated 9.5 million – however remember that many also live in the countryside, far, far away from the big cities.

262) Britain has an aging population, who are living longer. What does this directly impact?

A – Cost of pensions and health care

263) True or False: COVID-19 has had significant and unequal effects depending on where in the UK people live, their level of education, socioeconomic status, and health.

Answer – True, asked by the Government Office for Science to produce an independent review on the long-term societal impacts of COVID-19, The British Academy highlighted concerns including rising unemployment and growing health inequality.

264) Is it a legal requirement that men and women are not discriminated against because of their gender, their working status, or for any other reason?

A – Yes

265) Is it true that women in Britain comprise about half of the workforce, and on average leave high school with more qualifications than male graduates?

A – Yes

---- Religion ----

266) The UK is historically Christian. As of the 2011 Census, which was the largest identifying religion at 59% of the population?
A – Christian

267) True or False: There are various religious buildings across the UK, such as churches, mosques, temples, gurdwaras, and others.
Answer – True

268) True or False: Everyone has the legal right to choose to practise any religion, and also to practise no religion.
Answer – True

269) The Church of England is also known as:
C – The Anglican Church

270) Who is the head of the Church of England?
B – The Monarchy
Note: The monarch has the right to select the Archbishop as well as other senior church officials. However, usually, the choice is made by the Prime Minister and a committee appointed by the Church. Following in Queen Elizabeth's footsteps, King Charles is the current head of the Church of England.

271) Who governs the Church of Scotland (otherwise known as the Presbyterian Church)?
A – Ministers and Elders

272) Who governs the established official Welsh and Northern Irish Churches?
D – There is no established church in these two countries

273) **Which is the other biggest denomination of Christianity in the British Isles, aside from the Church of England (Anglican Church)?**
A – Roman Catholic

274) **Which is the Patron Saint Day of England?**
A – St. George's Day, on the 23rd of April

275) **Which is the Patron Saint Day of Wales?**
B – St. David's Day, on the 1st of March

276) **Which is the Patron Saint Day of Scotland?**
D – St. Andrew's Day, on the 30th of November

277) **Which is the Patron Saint Day of Northern Ireland?**
C – St. Patrick's Day, on the 17th of March

278) **True or False: St. George's Day is an official holiday in England.**
Answer – False, only Scotland and Northern Ireland have their Patron Saint Day as an official holiday

---- Customs and Traditions ----

279) **On which day does Christmas take place, celebrating the birth of Jesus Christ?**
D – 25th of December

280) **Which of the following things is NOT commonly carried out by families in the UK on Christmas day?**
D – Going swimming in the morning

281) True or False: Boxing Day is a public holiday that takes place the day before Christmas Day.

Answer – False, Boxing Day takes place a day after Christmas Day

282) Which other Christian festival is celebrated in the UK?

A – Easter

283) What is the religious significance of Easter?

B – It marks the death of Jesus Christ on Good Friday and his rising from the dead on Easter Sunday

284) What food do people typically consume on Shrove Tuesday?

C – Pancakes

285) The 40 days of Lent (beginning on Ash Wednesday) typically involves what?

B – Reflection and giving up some food types

286) Which gift is given at Easter, sometimes even by non-religious individuals?

D – Easter eggs

287) Diwali (the festival of lights) takes place in October or November and lasts for five days. It celebrates the victory of good over evil and the power of knowledge. Which religion is Diwali celebrated by?

B – Hindus and Sikhs

288) Hannukah is celebrated in November or December for eight days. Which religion is it celebrated by?

C – Jews

289) Eid al-Fitr celebrates what?

B – The end of Ramadan

290) **Eid ul Adha and Eid al-Fitr are celebrated by which religion?**
A – Muslims

291) **Vaisakhi involves parades, dancing and singing on the 14th of April each year, it is celebrated by which religion?**
B – Sikhs

292) **On which day does Valentine's Day take place in the UK?**
A – February 14

293) **True or False: Bank holidays have no religious significance, but banks and many other businesses are closed for the day.**
Answer – True

294) **True or False: Bank holidays take place in May, late May, early June, and August**
Answer – True

295) **On which day does April Fool's Day take place?**
A – April 1

296) **What do children not usually do for their mothers and fathers on Mothering Sunday and Father's Day?**
D – Ignore them

297) **Bonfire Night takes place on the 5th of November, people set off fireworks and burn large fires. Which 1605 event does this celebrate?**
A – Guy Fawkes attempting to burn down the Houses of Parliament

298) Remembrance Day, held on the 11th of November each year, is marked by what at 11am?
A – 2 minutes of silence

---- Sports in the UK ----

299) True or False: Many sports such as football, cricket, rugby, tennis, and golf started in Britain.
Answer – True

300) When did the UK most recently host the Olympic and Paralympic Games in East London?
D – 2012

301) How many times has the UK hosted the Olympic Games?
C – Three times
Note: The UK has hosted the Olympic Games in 1908, 1948 and 2012.

302) What did runner Roger Bannister achieve in 1954?
C – He ran a mile in under 4 minutes

303) Ian Botham played which sport?
A – Cricket

304) Steve Redgrave won gold medals in which sport?
C – Rowing

305) Dame Kelly Holmes won two gold medals in which sport?
B – Running

306) Chris Hoy won six Olympic gold medals in which sport?
B – Cycling

307) Mo Farah is a what?

B – A long-distance runner

308) Andy Murray is the first British man to win what since 1936?

A – A Tennis Grand Slam

309) Ellie Simonds was the youngest Paralympian at which games?

D – 2008

310) The Ashes is a famous cricket tournament featuring a series of matches played against which country?

D – Australia

311) Which is the UK's most popular sport?

C – Football

312) True or False: Many towns and cities in the British Isles have their own teams which they support and there are fierce rivalries between them.

Answer – True

313) In which year did England win the FIFA World Cup?

B – 1966

314) True or False: Rugby has three different official formats, those being Rugby Union, Rugby League, and Rugby Racing.

Answer – False, there are two formats – Rugby Union and Rugby League.

315) Which is the most well-regarded international rugby tournament in Europe?

B – The Six Nations

316) Which British sport holds a strong association with Royalty?
A – Horse racing

317) Golf can be traced back to which country and century?
C – 15th Century Scotland

318) Which is the most famous tennis tournament held in Britain?
B – Wimbledon

319) Sir Robin Knox-Johnston was the first person to do what?
B – Sail around the world, single-handedly and without stopping

320) Recent British Formula 1 winners of the World Championship do not include who?
B – Daniel Riccardo

---- Arts and Culture ----

321) Which eight-week musical event held by the BBC has been running since 1927?
D – The Proms

322) Which British classical music composer was the organist at Westminster Abbey?
B – Henry Purcell

323) Who composed 'The Planets'?
C – Gustav Holst

324) Which of these is not an example of a popular summer music festival in the UK?

C – Strawbury

325) True or False: London's west end is also known as 'Theatreland'.

Answer – True

326) In the UK, architecture is both old and beautiful. Many cathedrals from the Middle Ages still stand today in places like Durham, York, Canterbury, and Salisbury. In the late 1600s, which architect helped to envision the new St. Paul's Cathedral after the Great Fire of London?

A – Christopher Wren

327) In the 18th Century, which architect had a large influence on the city of Bath and the Royal Crescent?

B – Robert Adam

328) Which famous landscape architect devised the grounds in many country homes, such as Chatsworth House?

B – Lancelot 'Capability' Brown

329) Which London flower show aired annually on TV showcases garden designs from the British Isles around the world?

C – Chelsea Flower Show

330) True or False: Many great fashion icons come from the UK, some of these in recent years include Alexander McQueen and Vivienne Westwood.

Answer – True

331) True or False: St Pancras Station as well as town halls in Manchester and Sheffield are built in 'gothic' style architecture.

Answer – True

332) James Bond was introduced in which British author's book series.

B – Ian Fleming

333) Which famous English novelist wrote 'Sense and Sensibility' as well as 'Pride and Prejudice'?

A – Jane Austen

334) Which novelist wrote 'Oliver Twist' and 'Great Expectations'?

B – Charles Dickens

335) William Wordsworth wrote what?

B – Poems

336) Some of the best regarded poets are buried or remembered where in London?

A – Poets Corner

---- Leisure ----

337) What is the word for a garden that people in the UK can rent, which is not part of their home?

D – An allotment

338) Which flower is associated with England?

D – The rose

339) Which flower is associated with Scotland?

C – The thistle

340) Which flower is associated with Northern Ireland?

B – The shamrock

341) Which flower is associated with Wales?
A – The daffodil

342) What is the central shopping area of a town called?
A – The town centre

343) True or False: Many (but not all) families eat Yorkshire pudding with roast beef, gravy, potatoes, and vegetables on Sundays.
Answer – True

344) True or False: Haggis is a commonly consumed snack in England.
Answer – False, Haggis originates from and is popular in Scotland

345) In which year were films first shown publicly in the UK?
B – 1896

346) Which animated films were written by Nick Park?
B – Wallace and Gromit

347) True or False: Recent British actors to win Oscars include Kate Winslet and Colin Firth.
Answer – True

348) True or False: An important part of UK character is being able to laugh at ourselves, with comedy and satire.
Answer – True

349) What is the British equivalent of the Oscars?
A – The BAFTA's

350) Which of the following is a popular current soap opera TV show?

C – Coronation Street

351) Is it law that everybody watching television in the UK (whether on TV or a computer) must pay for a TV license?

A – Yes

352) If you watch TV without a license in the home, what is the maximum fine applicable?

D – £1,000

353) What does the money generated from the TV license fund?

A – The BBC

354) Which is NOT a popular social network that people in the UK use to keep in communication with each other?

D – WeChat

355) True or False: Playing darts, pool, drinking beer, and quizzes are traditional activities that British people do at public houses, or pubs as they are more widely known.

Answer – True

356) What is the drinking age in the UK to buy alcohol?

C – 18

357) What is the drinking age in the UK to buy alcohol when with a parent and eating a meal at the same time?

B – 16

358) True or False: Dog owners must ensure their dogs are wearing a collar showing their owner's name and address when out in public.

Answer – True

359) True or False: Pet owners are allowed to be cruel and neglectful in some scenarios.

Answer – False, it is against the law to treat a pet with cruelty

---- UK Places of Interest ----

360) The UK offers lots of outdoor spaces for mountain biking, mountaineering, camping, and hill walking. How many national parks are there in England, Scotland and Wales?

B – 15

361) What is the name of the popular clock at the Houses of Parliament in London?

B – Big Ben

362) Where is the Eden Project found?

D – Cornwall

363) In which country is the Giant's Causeway located?

D – Northern Ireland

364) When was the Giant's Causeway formed?

B – 50 million years ago

365) Loch Lomond is the largest body of fresh water in mainland Britain, which country is it located in?

B – Scotland

366) Snowdonia is a national park covering 823 square miles, which country is it located in?
C – Wales

367) Who was the Tower of London built after he was crowned King in 1066?
C – William The Conqueror

368) Which is England's largest national park?
B – The Lake District

369) The Lake District is famous for what?
D – Lakes and mountains

---- British Democracy and The Constitution----

370) In the democratic system, who gets a say in decisions that are made?
C – Only adults

371) In the 1830s and 40s, which group campaigned for reform of voting rights?
B – The Chartists

372) True or False: The British Constitution has been written down in a single document.
Answer – False, it is classed as 'unwritten', because there has never been a revolution such as in the United States of America or France.

373) True or False: The British Constitution contains laws, conventions as well as institutions responsible for leading the country.

Answer – True

374) Who is the current head of the Monarchy for the UK and other countries in the Commonwealth?

D – King Charles III

375) Under a constitutional monarchy, does the King or Queen decide government policy?

C – No, but he/she does communicate with and support the government

376) Who is the current heir to the throne?

D – Prince William

Note: As the eldest son of King Charles III, Prince William is the current heir, and not Charles's younger siblings or Queen Camilla.

377) What is the current national anthem of the UK?

A – God Save the King

The anthem reverted to the "King" version following the succession of Charles III as King in September 2022.

378) In which year did Queen Elizabeth II celebrate 70 years on the throne?

D – 2022

379) True or False: New citizens must affirm loyalty to the King or Queen as part of the citizenship ceremony.

Answer – True

380) What is the system of government defined as in the UK?

D – Parliamentary democracy

381) What are voters' regions called?

B – Constituencies

382) If two parties join due to a lack of majority, what is this type of government called? This most recently happened in 2010 with the Conservatives and Liberal Democrats.

C – A coalition

383) Why is the House of Commons thought to be more important than the House of Lords?

B – Because its members are elected

384) True or False: At present, do people who inherit the title of Lord automatically get to attend the House of Lords?

Answer – False, this was only allowed before 1999

385) True or False: The House of Commons actually has the strength to overpower the House of Lords.

Answer – True, but it is not often needed

386) Who chairs the debates in the House of Commons?

A – The Speaker

387) The Speaker does not represent a political party even though he/she is a member of Parliament. How is the Speaker chosen?

C – By secret MP ballot

388) What does the Speaker of the House do?

B – Ensures the debate rules are followed

389) How often is a general election held in the British Isles?

B – At least every 5 years

390) If a Prime Minister resigns during his or her reign, which election takes place?

D – A by-election

391) Which British politician served as Prime Minister of the United Kingdom after previously serving as Leader of the Conservative Party, Foreign Secretary, and Mayor of London?

A – Boris Johnson

---- The Government ----

392) What is the address of the Prime Minister?

B – 10 Downing Street

393) Who appoints the Cabinet?

A – The Prime Minister

394) What is the Chancellor of the Exchequer responsible for?

B – The economy

395) What is the opposition?

D – The second largest party in the House of Commons

396) The leader of the opposition also appoints Ministers, what are they called?

C – Shadow Ministers

397) True or False: Anyone over 18 can stand for an election, even if they are not representing one of the major political parties.

Answer – True

398) People not representing a major party but standing in the election are called what:

B – Independents

399) Which of these is not a major political party in the UK?

D – Scottish Greens

400) What do pressure or lobby groups do?

B – Try to influence policy

401) True or False: Civil Servants are members of the party which is leading at the time.

Answer – False, civil servants are neutral politically

402) What do civil servants not do?

D – Work for free

403) True or False: Local authorities (governments) are funded by the main government and by local taxes.

Answer – True

404) How many local authorities does London have?

D – 33

405) In which month do most local authority elections take place?

A – May

406) In which year was power devolved to give people in Wales, Scotland, and Northern Ireland more power to govern the matters which directly affect them?

B – 1997

407) What is the more accurate word for the Welsh Assembly?

A – The Senedd

408) True or False: The Senedd makes laws in 21 areas across education, housing, economics, and more. The Senedd can also pass laws on these topics without approval from the UK Parliament.
Answer – True

409) The Scottish Parliament was created in 1999. In which city can you find it?
D – Edinburgh

410) True or False: The Scottish Parliament members are also elected by proportional representation, they can vote on every matter.
Answer – False, they can vote on every matter except for those reserved by the UK Parliament.

411) When was the Northern Ireland Assembly created?
A – After the Belfast Agreement in 1998

412) There are MLAs (Member of the Legislative Assembly) in Northern Ireland, which of the following do they NOT make decisions on?
C – The Northern Ireland football squad

413) In which of the following countries has the UK previously used its power to suspend devolved assemblies?
B – Northern Ireland

414) Parliamentary decisions are recorded in which official reports?
C – Hansard

415) True or False: The UK has a free press meaning that newspapers are free from governmental control.

Answer – True

416) True or False: Media coverage must not be biased.

Answer – True

417) If you are allowed to vote, must you be on what is called the electoral register?

B – Yes

418) Electoral registration is sent out every September or October, what must you include when you send it back?

A – Names of eligible voters in the household

419) Where does voting take place when in the UK?

D – At polling stations

420) What time are polling stations open on Election Day?

A – 7am to 10pm

421) True or False: You can view the list of voters at the local authority/some libraries.

Answer – True, but it is supervised

422) True or False: Everybody has the right to try and convince you to vote for a specific candidate.

Answer – False

423) If you cannot attend the polling station (for example when on holiday), what should you do?

D – Send a postal vote

424) Which of the following CAN stand for office?
D – Over 18's in the UK

425) True or False: You can get free tickets to watch debates in the UK Parliament.
Answer – True, you can write to your local MP in advance or queue outside on the day

426) True or False: Voting in the UK is compulsory for citizens between 18 and 65 years old.
Answer – False, voting is not compulsory in the UK

---- The UK/ International Institutions ----

427) What is the current goal of the Commonwealth?
A – To work toward common goals and help each other

428) King Charles III is the head of the Commonwealth, which currently has how many states?
C – 56
Note: In 2022, the Commonwealth admitted Gabon and Togo as its 55th and 56th members respectively.

429) How much power does the Commonwealth have over its members?
B – None, but it can stop membership

430) Which of these is not a core value of the Commonwealth?
C – Freedom

431) True or False: Singapore is a member of the Commonwealth.
Answer – True

432) True or False: Switzerland is a member of the Commonwealth.
Answer – False

433) Which of these is not an international organisation of which the UK is a member?
D – The EU

434) The Council of Europe is most well-known for defending what?
B – Human rights

---- Respecting the Law ----

435) True or False: Every person in the UK receives equal treatment under the law, including non-citizens.
Answer – True

436) True or False: Criminal law is different from civil law as it only relates to crimes, rather than settling disputes.
Answer – True

437) Which of the following are NOT examples of illegal crimes?
C – Owing unpaid debt/money

438) Which of these is NOT an example of civil law?
B – Selling or buying drugs

439) The three general duties of the police are to protect life/ property, keep the peace, and prevent/detect crime. Which of the following is NOT true?
D – The police in the UK are also commonly known as the FBI

440) Who sets the local police budget?
D – The Police and Crime Commissioners (PCCs)

441) True or False: The police themselves must also obey the law.
Answer – True

442) True or False: Police Community Support Officers (PCSOs) have the power to arrest someone.
Answer – False

443) The UK faces terrorist threats, where are these supposedly from?
A – Al Qaida and Northern Ireland related groups

444) The Judiciary refers to what?
B – Judges

---- The Role of Courts ----

445) True or False: The Government must change the law if the Judiciary deem they have done something illegal.
Answer – True

446) When a public body is thought to have not respected somebody's rights, what are they usually ordered to do?
A – Pay compensation/change practises

447) In England, Wales, and Northern Ireland, minor criminal cases are usually dealt with at which court?
B – Magistrates Court

448) In Scotland, the same minor criminal cases are dealt with at which court?

A – Justice of the Peace Court

449) In England, Wales, and Northern Ireland, where are serious offences tried?

D – Crown Courts

450) In Scotland, where are serious criminal offences tried?

C – Sherriff Court

451) True or False: Magistrates and Justice of the Peace Judges do not need legal qualifications.

Answer – True

452) True or False: In Northern Ireland, small crimes are also decided by unqualified and unpaid Judges.

Answer – False, District Judges and Deputy District Judges in Northern Ireland are both paid and qualified

453) In all countries in the UK, for serious cases like murder, who is also present alongside the Judges?

A – A jury

454) What is a jury?

B – Members of the public chosen at random

455) True or False: Jury service is optional when you are asked to do it.

Answer – False, you have to go, unless you have a good reason not to

456) True or False: The jury decides on the penalty given to a criminal.

Answer – False, the Judge makes this decision

457) How many members are on the jury in Scotland?
C – 15

458) In England, Wales, or Northern Ireland, where would somebody ages 10 and 17 who committed a crime go to court?
B – Dedicated Youth Court

459) Which type of judge oversees cases at a Youth Court?
A – Specially trained Magistrates or a District Judge

460) If somebody in England, Wales, or Northern Ireland between ages 10 and 17 commits a serious crime, which court would they go to?
A – Crown Court

461) What is not allowed to be published about dealings in the court for people ages 10 and 17?
A – Names and photographs

462) Which court deals with civil disputes in England, Wales, and Northern Ireland?
D – The County Courts

463) Which of these matters would not be dealt with at a county court?
B – Armed robbery

464) For more serious civil matters, like when large amounts of money are being claimed as compensation – where could these be dealt with in England, Wales, and Northern Ireland?
A – The High Court

465) For more serious civil matters, like when large amounts of money are being claimed as compensation, where could these be dealt with in Scotland?

D – The Court of Session, which is in Edinburgh

466) True or False: The small claims procedure is for helping people settle minor disputes for amounts of money below £10,000 in England/Wales or below £3,000 in Scotland and Northern Ireland.

Answer – True

467) True or False: Solicitors are lawyers who can represent their clients.

Answer – True

---- Fundamental Principles ----

468) When did the UK sign the European Human Rights Convention?

B – 1950

469) Which of these is not part of the European Convention of Human Rights?

B – Driving your car at any speed

470) True or False: The UK is a place of equal opportunity for all.

Answer – True

471) True or False: Violence and brutality in the home is a serious offence.

Answer – True

472) Which of the following is acceptable in the UK?
B – Arranged marriage

473) If anybody is trying to force a marriage, they can go to jail for how long?
A – 2 years

---- Our Taxation----

474) What is the UK's stance on taxation?
A – Taxation is beneficial to society

475) People in the UK pay income tax from their employment, self-employment and income from some investments. What does this money help fund?
A – Roads, schools, the army, and more

476) True or False: Employed people pay tax via PAYE (Pay as you earn).
Answer – True

477) True or False: Self-employed people also pay taxes via PAYE.
Answer – False, they pay it themselves via self-assessment

478) True or False: Self-employed individuals are allowed to have their friends pay their tax liabilities on their behalf.
Answer – False, they must pay it themselves

479) What other tax must all working people in the UK contribute?
D – National Insurance

480) What does National Insurance fund?
B – State benefits

481) At what age do you receive a National Insurance number?
B – 16

---- UK Driving ----

482) What is the age at which you can learn to drive?
A – 17

483) True or False: Moped drivers can begin to learn at age 16.
Answer – True

484) True or False: The driving test in the UK includes only a theoretical test.
Answer – False, it includes a practical and a theoretical test in two parts

485) What must newly qualified drivers in Northern Ireland display?
B – A 'P' plate

486) For how long can you use a driving license from another country in the UK?
C – 12 months

487) What should you do if your vehicle is not being used?
D – Make a SORN (an off-road-notice)

488) Not having car insurance is a serious offence. If your vehicle is more than three years old, what must you do with your car every year?

D – Take it for a MOT Test
Note: 'MOT' stands for Ministry of Transport

---- Your Role in the Community ----

489) When you move to a new house or apartment, what is it custom to do?
B – Get to know your neighbours

490) Volunteering at schools is a good way to demonstrate what?
A – That you are a good citizen

491) Which of the following ways is NOT a standard way to help at a school?
D – Telling others in the community to join the same school

492) How should you approach becoming a school governor?
C – Apply online

493) True or False: You can join a political party and hand out leaflets for them – this is called canvassing.
Answer – True

494) True or False: There are also possibilities to help at local youth projects, universities, housing groups, museums, and more.
Answer – True

495) True or False: It is possible to volunteer with the police.
Answer – True

496) True or False: Giving blood takes less than an hour and can save countless lives of your fellow citizens.

Answer – True

497) **Which of these is NOT a tangible benefit you will get from volunteering?**

D – Earning money

498) **Which of these is not an example of volunteering?**

B – Delivering takeaway for Uber Eats

499) **True or False: There are also many charities you can volunteer with and donate to, for example, you can volunteer for Oxfam at Summer Music Festivals and receive a free ticket.**

Answer – True

500) **True or False: People aged 18 and under are also allowed to volunteer.**

Answer – True, they can for example volunteer with the National Citizen Service at 16 or 17

List of Kings and Queens

Year	Monarch	Year	Monarch
Saxon Kings		**House of York**	
871-899	Alfred the Great	1471-1483	Edward IV
899-925	Edward the Elder	1483	Edward V
925-939	Athelstan	1483-1485	Richard III
939-946	Edmund I	**House of Tudor**	
946-955	Eadred	1485-1509	Henry VII
955-959	Eadwig (Edwy)	1509-1547	Henry VIII
959-975	Edgar (The Peaceful)	1547-1553	Edward VI
975-978	Edward the Martyr	1553	Lady Jane Grey
978-1016	Ethelred II (The Unready)	1553-1558	Queen Mary I
1016	Edmund II (Ironside)	1558-1603	Queen Elizabeth I
1016-1035	Canute I	**House of Stewart**	
1035-1040	Harold I (Harefoot)	1603-1625	James I

1040-1042	Canute II (Hardicanute)	1625-1649	Charles I
1042-1066	Edward the Confessor	*1649-1660*	*Oliver Cromwell*
1066	Harold II	1660-1685	Charles II
Norman Kings		1685-1688	James II
1066-1087	William I (The Conqueror)	1689-1702	William III & Queen Mary II
1087-1100	William II	1702-1714	Queen Anne
1100-1135	Henry I	**House of Hanover**	
1135-1154	Stephen	1714-1727	George I
1141-1167	Express Matilda	1727-1760	George II
House of Plantagenet		1760-1820	George III
1154-1189	Henry II	1820-1830	George IV
1189-1199	Richard I (The Lionheart)	1830-1837	William IV
1199-1216	John	1837-1901	Queen Victoria
1216-1272	Henry III	1901-1910	Edward VII
1272-1307	Edward I	**House of Windsor**	
1307-1327	Edward II	1910-1936	George V
1327-1377	Edward III	1936	Edward VIII
1377-1399	Richard II	1936-1952	George VI
House of Lancaster		1952-2022	Queen Elizabeth II

1399-1413	Henry IV	2022-	King Charles III
1413-1422	Henry V		
1422-1461	Henry VI		
1461-1470	Edward IV		
1470-1471	Henry VI		

Important Sports Personalities

Roger Bannister – Ran a mile in under four minutes

Jessica Ennis Hill – Famous sportswoman and winner of Olympic gold medals

Tanni Grey-Thompson – Won 16 Paralympic medals, won London marathon six times

Kelly Holmes – Two gold medals for running, holds many records

Chris Hoy – Scottish cyclist, won six gold medals

Ellen Macarthur – Yachtswoman who became fastest to sail round the world solo

Bobby Moore – Captain of the English football team who won the World Cup

Andy Murray – Scottish Tennis player who won Britain's first Grand Slam since 1963. Also won Olympic gold.

Steve Redgrave – Famous rower for Britain

Ellie Simmonds – British Swimmer who won many gold medals, youngest member at 2008 Games

Jackie Stewart – Scottish Formula 1 driver. Won three Formula 1 Championships.

Jayne Torvill and Christopher Dean – Won gold medals for figure skating at the 1984 Olympics

David Weir – Six gold medals over two games – won London Marathon six times

Bradley Wiggins – Cyclist and first Brit to win the Tour De France, winner of eight Olympic gold medals

Important Cultural Personalities
(Artists and Writers)

David Allan – Known for 'The Origin of Painting'

Jane Austen – English novelist who wrote Sense and Sensibility

John Constable – Landscape painter, famous for raising the profile of this style

Charles Dickens – Wrote 'Oliver Twist' and 'Great Expectations'

Thomas Gainsbourough – Portrait painter

Thomas Hardy – Author and Poet who wrote 'Far from the madding crowd'

John Lavery – Successful Northern Irish painter who painted the Royal Family

Henry Moore – English artist known for his bronze sculptures

John Pett – Welsh artist known for engravings and stained glass

JK Rowling – Wrote the 'Harry Potter' series to huge global success

Eveyln Waugh – Wrote satirical novels known for Brideshead Revisited

20th Century British Inventors

ATM – James Goodfellow in 1967

Concorde – Supersonic jet by Britain and France in 1969

DNA Molecule – Discovered by Francis Crick and James Watson in 1953

Hovercrafts – Chris Cockerell in the 1950s

Jet Engines – Frank Whittle in the 1930s

Radar – Sir Robert Watson Watt

Television – John Logie Beard in the 1920s

Turing Machine – Alan Turing in the 1930s

World Wide Web – Tim Berners Lee at the start of the 90s

Ingram Content Group UK Ltd.
Milton Keynes UK
UKHW012119270423
420897UK00004B/177